Plays for Children 2

The Honoured Guest
by Debjani Chatterjee

Danny 306 + Me (4ever)
by David Greig

Stepping Stones
by Mike Kenny

Jumping on My Shadow
by Peter Rumney

With a Foreword by Alan Ayckbourn

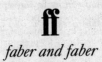

faber and faber

First published in 2004
by Faber and Faber Limited
3 Queen Square London WC1N 3AU
Published in the United States by Faber and Faber Inc.
an affiliate of Farrar, Straus and Giroux LLC, New York

Typeset by Country Setting, Kingsdown, Kent CT14 8ES
Printed in England by Mackays of Chatham plc, Chatham, Kent

A CIP record for this book
is available from the British Library

ISBN 0-571-22080-0

2 4 6 8 10 9 7 5 3 1

Contents

Biographical Notes on the Authors

Debjani Chatterjee has written, edited and translated over thirty-five books for children as well as for adults. She is one of the best-known Asian poets writing in Britain today. Her recent collections for children include *Animal Antics* and *Rainbow World: Poems from Many Cultures*. Debjani has also co-edited several bilingual books of poetry, stories and oral history – most recently *Daughters of a Riverine Land* and *Who Cares? Reminiscences of Yemeni Carers*. She is Chair of the National Association of Writers in Education, Vice-Chair of the Bengali Women's Support Group and an active member of Mini Mushaira. She has enjoyed a number of residencies including a Poetry Society-sponsored poetry residency at Sheffield Children's Hospital in 2000. In 2002 Sheffield Hallam University awarded her an honorary doctorate for her 'outstanding contribution to literature, the arts and community service'.

David Greig was born in Edinburgh in 1969 and now lives in Fife. His previous work for young people includes *Dr Korcak's Example* and *Petra's Explanation* (for TAG Theatre Company). His other plays include *San Diego*, *Outlying Islands*, *The Cosmonaut's Last Message*, *Victoria*, *The Speculator*, and *The Architect* and *Europe*. He also co-founded Suspect Culture, with whom he has written the texts and collaborated on many productions including *Casanova*, *Mainstream* and *Timeless*.

Mike Kenny has written over sixty plays, mostly for a children's or family audience. *Stepping Stones* was the Writers' Guild of Great Britain Best Children's Play in

1997, and he was the first ever recipient of the Arts Council of England's Children's Award in 2000. His plays include *Bag Dancing*, *The Lost Child*, *Walking the Tightrope*, and adaptations of traditional tales such as *Rumpelstiltskin* and *Scheherezade*. He is currently Writer in Residence at Birmingham Rep and teaches regularly at York Steiner School.

Peter Rumney is an actor, director, writer, community artist, arts administrator, and university lecturer. His plays include: *Moving Voices* (for Theatre Centre, 1995; then Wolsey TIE, 1996; Sheffield Crucible and Mersyside YPT, 1999), *The Man Who Planted Trees* (New Perspectives, 1996), *White Feathers* (Gazebo, 1997, then MYPT, 2004), *The Rock* (Theatr Iolo, 1998), *Jumping on my Shadow* (Theatre Centre, 2001), *Beyond the Wall and Over the Sea* (Haymarket Leicester, 2001) and *Dragon Breath* (Made 2 Measure/Creative Partnerships/Nottingham Trent University, 2004). Winner, Arts Council of England John Whiting Award for Best Play, 2002. He is particularly interested in working with groups who might consider themselves marginalised or disenfranchised by mainstream culture, such as people with disabilities; refugees; the elderly; and younger children with emotional and behavioural difficulties. Most of his plays have been written for young people, and he likes to work with his potential audience to create the themes, images and characters that inhabit the performances.

Foreword

After thirty years writing exclusively for adults, it was
only in 1988 that I began seriously to consider the
prospect of creating something specifically for a younger
audience.

I sensed a gap at the time that I felt badly needed
addressing – namely, that there was precious little 'serious'
theatre writing being done for younger children either
for them to watch or to perform. Apart from any other
consideration I became conscious, too, as the long-
serving artistic director of a regional company, that
as a result of this neglect we were actively discouraging
our future audience.

I set about trying to remedy this. Fifteen years and
a dozen plays later, I have had no regrets. Frankly, the
rewards of such writing (when you manage to pull it off!)
beat anything you're ever going to get from the most
elevated West End opening.

The theatrical act of live performance, that special
moment of 'now' when live actor meets audience is
unique in any circumstance; in children's theatre it is
intensified tenfold. They become almost tangible, those
threads of trust woven between the two parties, as the
performer presents, demands, persuades and cajoles the
spectators, drawing them into the web of narrative and
character which the author has created. Yet this strength
is also brittle. One false step in performance, one small,
untruthful concession to the pre-established rules and all
is lost – sometimes for ever. Quick curtain – home time.

Theatre, particularly amongst our national leaders all
of whom are old enough to know better, has seemingly

been dismissed as irrelevant to the upbringing of our bright young twenty-first- century high-tech children. I believe, on the contrary, that the reverse is true. Live theatre is more, much, much more important than it has ever been.

True, we have achieved technological miracles with the graphics and sound which fill all our screens – images that are sometimes literally jaw dropping. But in the end these are, after all, the finite imaginings of others not ourselves. There isn't, at the end of it, very much left for us to do. Instead, we become reactive rather than inter-reactive. Like a puzzle book with all the answers printed next to the questions, there is never a moment when we are asked if we would like to contribute. It has all been decided long ago by people we will never meet, living in places we are probably never likely to visit.

Whatever happened to the infinitely possible?

Which is why I welcome this latest book. Here are four plays that don't, indeed cannot, provide all the answers. Varied, exciting, adventurous in their horizons, they wait, expectantly like good plays should, now passive texts, for the moment to activate, the instant when performer meets audience and the air will once again be thick with wondrous imaginings for both. It's a magic time.

Treasure it.

Alan Ayckbourn
Scarborough, October 2003

THE HONOURED GUEST

Debjani Chatterjee

The Honoured Guest was first presented as a touring production by Twisting Yarn Theatre on 27 November 2000. The cast was as follows:

Kobi Kabir Moey Hassan
Serving Woman Sally Austen
Lady Sharifa Snobbyshowoff Shahzada Tina Ellicott
Messenger Sally Austen
Gatekeeper One Tina Ellicott
Gatekeeper Two Sally Austen

Director Iain Bloomfield
Designer Jeremy Nicholls
Costumes and Puppets Naomi Parker, Sarah Worrall
Administration Su Holgate

Characters

Kobi Kabir

The multilingual poet/storyteller/narrator and
protagonist. 'Kobi' is the Bengali word for poet.
He is very confident about his skill with words and
is observant and full of curiosity. He has two sets
of costumes: a simple patchwork robe that could have
the alphabet in various languages painted in purple
or sewn on, and a gorgeous glittering costume which
he wears to the feast. The latter is a voluminous
multi-coloured robe with many deep pockets. Opulent
jewellery, a big turban, a great sword in a colourful
scabbard and shiny *nagra* shoes with huge toe-curls
complete the latter ensemble. Both robes have
full skirts that billow out when he pirouettes.

Serving Woman

A pretty woman, but plainly dressed in a dull
(perhaps beige) cotton *salwar-kameez*. She works
for the Lady Sharifa Snobbyshowoff Shahzada
as her cook as well as personal maid.

Lady Sharifa Snobbyshowoff Shahzada

An extremely rich and fastidious lady who lives
in a marble palace and has gorgeous saris to wear.
She loves showing off her wealth by throwing parties
for the rich and famous, and is always greedy
for flattery and presents. She fawns on those who
are extremely wealthy and famous, but is mean to
the poor and to those who work for her.

Messenger

A colourful character, resembling a town crier, he is
full of airs and graces, and given to dramatic gestures.
He is richly costumed, made up in Kathakali dance style,
and carries a *dumaru* (a tiny Indian drum) in one hand.
Messenger has a loud sonorous voice and loves to repeat
himself and to have others repeat his words. He works
for the Lady Sharifa Snobbyshowoff Shahzada and
also acts as her punkah wallah and handyman.

Gatekeepers One and Two

Mustachioed men who look comical in their over-the-top
eastern-style uniforms of glittering red and gold.
They both wear red and gold open waistcoats and
very ostentatious gold *nagra* slippers with great
exaggerated toe-curls at the front. Gatekeeper One
is a fidgety man. He is very thin and tall and wears
a ridiculously large green turban and a monstrously
big moustache that curls up at the ends. His skin-tight
pantaloons are striped red and green, and his waistcoat
is far too big for him. He sports a long red *tika* on his
forehead. Gatekeeper Two is fond of food and sleep.
He is very fat and short and wears a tiny green fez
with long gold tassels on his head. He sports a little
Charlie Chaplin moustache, a pigtail tied with a red
ribbon, and has a very large red dot on his forehead.
He wears extremely baggy green harem trousers,
decorated with large red spots. Both Gatekeepers
tend to use artificial and singsong voices when
talking to important guests.

Guests at the Feast

These, including Guests One and Two, will be
the children in the audience, all wearing costumes
and carrying presents (elaborately wrapped boxes
and parcels).

Act One

The spotlight falls centre stage, where Kobi Kabir is sitting cross-legged, writing with great concentration. Then he looks up at the audience, surprised.

Kobi Kabir Ah! There you are, my friends, *mes amis, méré yaron, amar bondhura. (He scrambles to his feet.)* I was so busy spinning yarns in so many languages that I didn't notice you for a moment. Greetings. *Namasté. Salaam aléikum. Bonjour. Kombaawa. Hola. Ciao. Ghudyambo.* Top of the morning to you! What! You don't know me, Kobi Kabir – (*Does a pirouette, the skirt of his robe fanning out around him.*) – the multilingual Bard of Bardford – (*Does another pirouette.*) – the Poet Laureate of Kahanistan – (*Does yet another pirouette.*) – the brightest Jewel at the Court of Maharaja Vikramaditya? (*He does a double pirouette and flops down, dizzy. Then, scrambling to his feet:*) But I know you, my friends – you are my audience, my readers, my listeners. So listen and I'll tell you who I am. *Achha?* Okay?

I am a great poet,

> *Drum roll.*

Ami moha kobi,

> *Drum roll.*

I write all kinds of verse:

> *Flute notes.*

nana chhora likhi,

7

Flute notes.

stories, poems, letters,

Sitar tune.

golpo, kabbo, chhiti,

Sitar tune.

I recite them all.

Shahnai note.

Shob kori abritti.

Shahnai note.

There is such power in the pen!

Drum roll.

Kolomér achhé kee shokti!

Drum roll.

There is such power in the pen!

Drum roll.

Kolomér achhé kee shokti!

Drum roll.

Now I made that one up on the spot. But do you want to know what it is that I was writing just now? *Achha,* here's a little sample.

Dékho! Look – (*Points.*) – *Daén dékho.* Look to my right.

The right side of the stage is lit up in a glaring red light.

Under the shade of a tamarind tree, a woman sits in the blistering heat, chopping the chillies and grinding the coriander and the cumin to be eaten at the feast . . .

Serving Woman wipes her brow.

Now *dékho! Baén dékho.* Look – (*Points.*) – to my left.

The left side of the stage is lit up in a soft cool blue-green light.

In the marbled cool of the palace, a lady sits in the calm, nimbly twisting the yarn that will provide the thread of a story to be told at the feast . . .

Gentle sitar music in the background. Then the light on both the left and the right side of the stage fades out and only the spotlight on centre stage remains.

Achha, you're probably wondering: *kya yéh kahani such hai? Ei golpo ki shotthi?* Is this a true story? That's a question I'm often asked. Well, of course it's true. Would I, Kobi Kabir, tell a lie? Here's the story then, exactly as it happened – er – exactly as I remember it, at this moment in time. But you will see it for yourself and you will judge the truth of it. For you too, my friends –

Points at the audience and the light falls on them.

– are in this story. It's the story of clothes – rich and poor – and it's the story of a feast – a feast given by the lady in the palace, the Lady Sharifa Snobbyshowoff Shahzada –

The blue-green light falls on the lady, who is now being helped by the Serving Woman to dress in a gorgeous sari.

– who is a very rich person indeed – a feast which her poor serving maid helps to cook and to serve – a feast which we will all attend. But first, *suno* – listen to the Messenger.

Messenger (*comes dancing in dramatically in Kathakali style, anklets jingling and* dumaru *beating*) Hear ye, hear ye. *Suno, suno.* Ladies and gentlemen of Kahanistan, *Kahanistan ké shrimaan-shrimati, khawateen-o-hazraat*, the Lady Sharifa Snobbyshowoff Shahzada is giving a feast. *Attention, attention, s'il vous plaît!* You there, attention please! Now, who did I say was doing what?

Kobi Kabir The Lady Sharifa Snobbyshowoff Shahzada is giving a feast.

Messenger *Achha*, yes, that's right, I said a FEAST, an absolutely marvellous banquet, a most stupendous spread of delicious food and drink. And it's all happening tomorrow, *kal, kaalké, bokra, demain*. Now then, *when* did I say it's happening?

Kobi Kabir It's all happening tomorrow, *kal, kaalké, bokra, demain.*

Messenger *Shabaash*! Bravo! Well done! Oh, I do like to hear my words repeated back to me! The Lady Sharifa Snobbyshowoff Shahzada is giving a feast. And it's all happening tomorrow, *kal, kaalké, bokra, demain.* Oh what splendid feasts she gives! She employs the best cooks from all over the world. They make delicious dishes from every land and the sherbets are out of this world! (*He kisses the tips of his fingers.*)

Kobi Kabir So tell us, Messenger, where is the Lady Sharifa Snobbyshowoff Shahzada showing off her – er – I mean giving her magnificent feast?

Messenger Where else but at the Lady Sharifa Snobbyshowoff Shahzada's magnificent marble palace, of course! It's pretty as a picture, so picture a perfect party at the prettiest palace. There was never a *mahal* more magnificent or more beautifully marbled. It was modelled on the fabulous Taj Mahal itself and the Lady Sharifa Snobbyshowoff Shahzada has named it after her favourite celebrity, none other than – (*A dramatic pause and his* dumaru *rolls suspense*.) – herself, the Shahzada Mahal! (*He pauses*.) What did I say was the name of her palace?

Kobi Kabir The Shahzada Mahal.

Messenger That's right! Its pillars are carved with exotic trees and fantastic flowers and birds, its doors and windows are draped with richly embroidered silk curtains, there are cool fountains in the courtyards, peacocks dance in the gardens, the floors are decorated with colourful *rangoli* designs or *alpona* patterns and have many brocade cushions on which to sit and there are punkah wallahs to fan the guests in each of the spacious halls. So, where is the Lady Sharifa Snobbyshowoff Shahzada giving her magnificent feast?

Kobi Kabir Ah, at the Lady Sharifa Snobbyshowoff Shahzada's magnificent marble palace, the Shahzada Mahal. Eh, it must be a dream of a place to visit! And the thought of the delicious food and drink is enough to make my mouth water –

Quick flute note.

– and my tummy rumble.

Quick drum roll.

So tell us quickly, *jaldi batao*, Messenger, are we all invited to the Lady Sharifa Snobbyshowoff Shahzada's magnificent feast?

Messenger Don't be silly! The Lady Sharifa Snobby- showoff Shahzada only invites the high and the mighty, the great and the good, the royalty and the nobility: in short, only the rich and the powerful from all over the world – the celebrities, the movie stars, the pop singers, the football millionaires, the VIPs. So anyone who fits *that* description can come.

Kobi Kabir So does that mean us?

Messenger You? Don't be silly! You can't believe that the Lady Sharifa Snobbyshowoff Shahzada will mix with every Tom, Dick and Harry, every Ram, Sham and Ali. You're a nobody – you can't come. But (*looking at the audience*) as for the others at this place – yes, I see some very rich and important people here, so they will be welcome, of course. But don't forget, all who come must bring a magnificent present – the Lady Sharifa Snobbyshowoff Shahzada just adores receiving presents. What is it she just adores?

Kobi Kabir The Lady Sharifa Snobbyshowoff Shahzada just adores receiving presents. But don't you think it's not quite fair that –

Messenger Don't be silly! I'm not here to think. Now I'd better be on my way – there are so many more wonderful places that I must go to, so many more rich and famous people that I must invite to the Lady Sharifa Snobbyshowoff Shahzada's most magnificent feast. Ooh, it will be the talk of the town! *Adios, amigos. Au revoir.*

The Messenger dances away in Kathakali style, anklets jingling.

Kobi Kabir (*sitting down and talking to the audience*) *Achha*, the Lady Sharifa Snobbyshowoff Shahzada's feast is for *khoob dhoni aar bishishto loke*, the very rich and the important, and not for a nobody like me. (*jumping up*) But I would love to go and see her magnificent marble palace – *Taj Mahal jaisa sundar, Shahzada Mahal* – (*sighing*) – *hai!* – and eat the delicious food that they will be serving. Mmm, the thought of the delicious food and drink is enough to make my mouth water –

Quick flute note.

– and my tummy rumble

Quick drum roll.

I wonder what I can do? (*Thinks.*) I know! There are different kinds of rich people. There are those who are rich in money and have lots of gold and silver and costly clothes and jewellery to wear. Then there are others who have little or no money, but they may be rich in other ways. Some people are rich in their friends because they have many good friends, some are rich in their children and have good and wonderful children, and then there are some who are rich in having special talents. So I too am rich, for I am rich in words and in languages. *Mai ék nazm – ék kavita – likhunga, ami aik kobita likhbo,* I will write a poem to the Lady Sharifa Snobbyshowoff Shahzada and she will see for herself what a magnificent present a poem can be. And besides, there's no one who is a nobody – we are all somebodies, *hai na?* Aren't we? We are all important to someone or the other, *hai na?* I *will* go to the party with you after all! (*He performs a pirouette and a few ballet skips.*)

Act Two

The two Gatekeepers, looking grand in their red and gold glittering uniforms, are on either side of a very impressive arched gateway. Gatekeeper One stands to one side of the gate and engages himself in skipping about and shadow-boxing, looking quite fiercely at an imaginary enemy. Every now and then he grunts and gives a karate chop or lands a boxing punch, then jumps up looking delighted with himself. Gatekeeper Two is sitting down and snoring; his mouth is open and he occasionally mumbles in his sleep. Kobi Kabir stands at one side of the stage and talks to the audience. The Gatekeepers are unaware of him.

Kobi Kabir There is just an hour to go before the Lady Sharifa Snobbyshowoff Shahzada's guests start arriving. (*pointing*) *Dékho*, how magnificently the gateway to the Shahzada Mahal is decorated! *Aur yéh bhi dékho*, how smartly she has dressed her gatekeepers. Her feast is certainly all about dress. *Lekin yéh do buddhu kya kar rahé hai?* But what are these two idiots up to? One of them fancies himself a martial arts expert.

Gatekeeper One Cor! Just another hour to kill. And some more scum deserving of punishment. Pow! Take that! Wow! And that! So die all my enemies. Hah! I'm the bravest of the brave! What powerful muscles I have! These mighty hands of mine are lethal weapons! Le-ee-thal weapons! And when I kick someone's butt – (*giving a mighty kick demonstration*) – he'll be orbiting in space before he knows it! (*addressing his companion*) I say, matey, did you see that? My fist is like lightning. I've flattened our enemies in no time at all.

Kobi Kabir But the snoring gatekeeper is unimpressed. He is dreaming of the food at the feast. (*He puts a hand to one ear.*) Suno!

Gatekeeper Two (*talking rhythmically in his sleep*) *Pulaoér pahar! Biryanir bahar! Khathaaler jhol! Golapi gondhé ghol! Aloo bhaja, doi bora! Laoo kumro! Machhér muro! Shag shobji! Tatka chingri! Mottoshuti phoolkopi! Roshogolla aar jilebee! Chom chom aar aloor dom! Kee moja halwa!* Yum, yum, yummy, yummy! *Kee moja* in my tummy! Yum, yum, yummy, yummy! All the food goes in my tummy!

Gatekeeper One Hey, Sleeping Beauty! Wakey, wakey, rise and shine. (*He bends and shouts into his snoring companion's ear.*) Hey, are you with us, sunshine?

Gatekeeper Two (*scrambling to his feet*) *Nishchoi! Nishchoi!* (*rubbing his ear*) *Ato joré chitkaar korbar kono dorkar nei, ami shob shunté parchhi.* Umm . . . ? *Tumi kee bollé?*

Gatekeeper One I had to shout, bro, because you were talking so loudly in your sleep. You've even made me forget what I was saying just now!

Gatekeeper Two (*shaking his pigtailed head*) *Na, na, motei na! Ami to jege chhilam atokkhoo-oo-n dhore!*

Gatekeeper One (*stabbing at Gatekeeper Two with an accusing finger*) You wide awake? As if! You *were* fast asleep; you were snoozing and napping, you were in the Land of Nod and Beddy-byes, taking forty winks. You were in the arms of Morpheus, you were dead to the world, you were sleeping like a log, you were . . .

Gatekeeper Two (*shaking his pigtailed head*) Na, na, motei na! Motei na!

Gatekeeper One (*stabbing at Gatekeeper Two with an accusing finger*) Oh yes you were.

> *He indicates to the audience to join in with him in shouting 'Oh yes you were.' But Gatekeeper Two keeps denying it: 'Na, na, motei na!' The two Gatekeepers argue inaudibly in the background while Kobi Kabir steps forward to talk to the audience.*

Kobi Kabir Behind me are the highly trained gatekeepers of the Lady Sharifa Snobbyshowoff Shahzada.

> *By now the Gatekeepers are thumping each other.*

But enough of this stupid thumping of each other! (*Kobi Kabir flourishes a hand, magician-style, turns a pirouette and skips back to the side of the stage.*)

Gatekeeper One I say, flower, enough of this bickering. It's still a while before the Lady Sharifa Snobbyshowoff Shahzada's guests arrive. Have you any bright ideas about how we could pass the time?

Gatekeeper Two (*rubbing his hands with glee*) Nishchoi! Nishchoi! Shundori Shrimoti Sharifa Snobbyshowoff Shahzada kee opurbo khabar khawabe othithhider! Amritor moto khabar!

Gatekeeper One Oh no, not food again!

Gatekeeper Two Amra khabarer ak talika korte pari.

> *He rubs his tummy, rolls his eyes and pronounces rhythmically:*

Pulaoér pahar! Biryanir bahar! Khatthaaler jhol! Golapi gondhé ghol! Aloo bhaja, doi bora! Laoo kumro! Machhér muro! Shag shobji! Tatka chingri! Mottoshuti

*phookopi! Roshogolla aar jilebee! Chom chom aar aloor
dom! Kee moja halwa!* (*Chuckles.*) Yum, yum, yummy,
yummy! *Kee moja* in my tummy! Yum, yum, yummy,
yummy! All the food goes in my tummy!

Gatekeeper One Just listen to yourself, chuck! This long
list of food is what you've been muttering all the time in
your sleep. How do you even know what food has been
prepared for the feast? And anyway, blockhead, what
does it matter what wonderful dishes the guests will eat?
You can be sure that we gatekeepers won't be fed in such
royal style. Our employer is well known to be very mean
with all those who work for her.

Gatekeeper Two (*smirking coyly*) *Eito tomar bhool.
Shundori Shrimoti Sharifa Snobbyshowoff Shahzadar oti
shundor aar doyalu jhee amay pochhondo koré!*

Gatekeeper One Oooohhh! So you're pally with Her
Ladyship's serving maid?

Gatekeeper Two *Shé amae boléchhé ki ki khabar to-uri
koréchhé aar shé amadér jonno khabar tulé rékhéchhé.*

Gatekeeper One Okey-dokey, nice one, chuff! So we'll
get well fed after all. I wish we could always enjoy her
cooking! Anyway, it won't be until after the feast is over
that we can eat, so it's best we keep our minds off food
for now. Hmm . . . (*Thinks.*)

Gatekeeper Two (*gloomily nods agreement*) *Theek
bolecho.* Hmm . . .

Kobi Kabir (*stepping forward again*) Messenger has
been training these gatekeepers of the Lady Sharifa
Snobbyshowoff Shahzada to greet important guests from
all over the world, using the language and the customs
of those people. It might be fun to see how well they've
learnt. (*Kobi Kabir flourishes a hand at the two guards,*

magician-style, turns a pirouette and walks back to the side of the stage.)

Gatekeeper Two *(excitedly)* *Aré hai! Amra jé shob training péyéchi, nana bhashae desh-bidesher othithhider shagot kora – sheshober ektu* practise *hoye jaak! Kee bolo?*

Gatekeeper One Practise welcoming guests from all over the world? Great stuff! That sleep's done you good – it's got your brain working. But I tell you what – *I'll* be the one to test you!

Gatekeeper Two *(shakes his head violently, pigtail flying) Na, na, khobordar na! Éta ami bhebechi, tai ami tomai proshno korbo! Ami tomar porikkha nebo!*

Gatekeeper One No, I'll be the one to test you!

Gatekeeper Two *(shakes his head violently) Na, na! Ami.*

> *The Gatekeepers bicker for a bit, then they pull faces at each other. After a while, Gatekeeper One pulls Gatekeeper Two's pigtail and then runs around the stage being chased by his angry little companion. When they run around the audience, Kobi Kabir steps forward.*

Kobi Kabir Oof! Enough of this stupidity! *(He flourishes a hand, magician-style, turns a pirouette and walks back to the side of the stage.)*

Gatekeeper Two *(stops running and puts up his hands in a gesture of surrender) Achha, achha! Onik hoyeche! Thhamo ebar. Theek achhe, tumi amar porikkha nebe aar ami tomar. Kamon?*

Gatekeeper One *(also stopping)* Right you are then! We'll *both* test each other. Why didn't you say so in the first place?

Gatekeeper Two *Achha, baba, achha!* (*A sly look comes on his round face.*) *Amra dujonei porikkha nebo, kintu ami agé!*

Gatekeeper One You rascal! You always have to be the first, haven't you!

Thumps him and is thumped back. Gatekeeper One jumps on his foot and Gatekeeper Two hops about in agony while Gatekeeper One laughs. Then Gatekeeper Two pinches Gatekeeper One on his backside. This results in Gatekeeper One giving chase. Kobi Kabir shrugs his shoulders and throws up his hands. The two gatekeepers chase each other around the stage and the audience until they meet again in front of the gate. Kobi Kabir again flourishes a hand, magician-style, turns a pirouette and walks back to the side of the stage. The two Gatekeepers bump into each other and fall down.

Gatekeepers One *and* **Two** Sorry! Oh, let's start again.

Gatekeeper One (*bowing politely*) You first, love.

Gatekeeper Two (*bowing politely*) Na, na, prothomé apni.

They both bow a few times, each bowing lower than the other until both fall down.

Gatekeeper One Righto! Stand up straight then. Here I come.

He comes jumping about and clapping on his mouth while ululating, Red Indian fashion. Gatekeeper Two also jumps about with both hands joined above his head, like a victorious boxer.

Gatekeeper Two I am the Champion! *Olé, olé!* I am the Champion!

Gatekeeper One *How*, idiot? *How?*

Gatekeeper Two (*howling*) I am the Champion Idiot! *Olé olé!* I am the Champion Idiot!

Gatekeeper One No, no! I know you're an idiot, but can't you see that I'm pretending to be a Red Indian? You were supposed to give me the Red Indian greeting. (*demonstrating with right hand up*) How!

Gatekeeper Two (*shrugging his shoulders*) *Ami kee koré ta janbo? Motéi Red Indian dakhachhé na!* (*lifting his right hand up, palm facing Gatekeeper One*) How!

Gatekeeper One Well, let's try another one.

Gatekeeper Two *Accha.*

> *He bends his knees slightly and strikes up a fierce attitude with his eyes rolling and tongue sticking out as a Maori might do when performing the* haka.

Gatekeeper One Stop messing about. Just because I called you an idiot, you don't have to pull faces at me.

> *But Gatekeeper Two continues to look very fierce and advances on him.*

Aha! So it's another test, is it, me old mucker?

> *He does a flying rugby tackle, pulls down Gatekeeper Two and proceeds to give him some karate chops.*

Gotcha, you evil gate-crashing enemy!

Gatekeeper Two *Aré, bokaram! Amai chinté parcho na? Ami holam New Zealand théké Maori. Amar haka dékhé bujhté parchona?*

Gatekeeper One (*shamefaced*) Oh, oh! That was your Maori haka greeting! I thought you were some evil enemy warrior. But I hardly think, you dum-dum, that a Maori warrior is likely to come to the Lady Sharifa Snobbyshowoff Shahzada's feast!

Gatekeeper Two *Nischoi hoté paré! America théké Red Indianra jodhi ashté paré, to New Zealand théké Maori lok-o ashté paré.*

Gatekeeper One Okay, come here, ducky. You'll never guess this greeting. *Hi!*

He rubs his nose against that of Gatekeeper Two.

Gatekeeper Two *Jani, jani. Eto phorashider babohar. Bonjour, bonjour. Comment allez-vous?*

He embraces the astonished Gatekeeper One and gives him a hearty kiss on both cheeks.

Gatekeeper One Hey, I gave you an Eskimo greeting, pal, and it's a warm and friendly nose-rub alright for a cold land, but there was no need for you to be slobbering all over me. Do you think we'll get a lot of French guests? Maybe a *Conte* and *Contestant*, or even a *Marquis* and *Marionette*! The Middle Eastern ones kiss too, don't they? A few sheikhs would really shake up the joint.

Gatekeeper Two *Eskimodér nak chhoa! Kojon Eskimo othithi ashé dékhi! Achha, achha! Ebar amar bari.*

He takes up the stance of a Japanese sumo wrestler, stamping first on one foot and then on the other. Gatekeeper Two copies him. Then both bow.

Gatekeeper One *Kombawa!* (*He bows low.*)

Gatekeeper Two *Kombawa!* (*He bows still lower.*) *Kombawa!*

Gatekeeper One *Kombawa!*

Each tries to bend lower than the other; then as they rise they knock their heads together and fall down.

Gatekeepers One *and* **Two** Ouch!

They rub their heads.

Act Three

In a cool courtyard of the Shahzada Mahal is a lovely fountain. Messenger sits by the fountain and polishes ornate brassware with a cloth. He is working hard and wipes the perspiration on his forehead. All around the courtyard are painted flowerpots and tubs with exotic flowers growing in them. Serving Woman enters from one side, carrying garden scissors and a flower basket.

Messenger (*looking up from his work*) What, still *more* flowers? Isn't she satisfied with all the armfuls you've already picked?

Serving Woman (*sighing*) You know that Snobby is never satisfied.

Messenger (*concerned*) That she-monster works you too hard. It makes my blood boil when I see how she treats you. I know you've been slaving away in the kitchen for ages. You're the one who cooks a fabulous feast and Her Snobbiness doesn't even thank you! Instead, she pretends that she employs the topmost chefs from all around the world! (*mimicking the Lady Sharifa Snobbyshowoff Shahzada*) 'This exquisite *coq au vin* is a work of art created by my French chef, Jean-Paul of Paris; these fresh and delicate slices of *sushi* are specially prepared by my Japanese chef, Michiko of Hokkaido; and this magnificent *mulakhayya* is a masterpiece made by none other than my Moroccan cook, Maroof of Marrakesh!'

> *Serving Woman laughs and curtsies at each name. Messenger then reverts to his normal voice.*

Her meanness and her hypocrisy are sickening! Oh I long to see the day when someone will teach her a lesson. Tell me, don't you want to get away from such a monstrous person?

Serving Woman Of course I dream of running away, but how would I get another job without a good reference from her? (*Sighs.*) She is hard on everyone who works for her. Look at yourself. She makes you run errands for her, carry her messages and invitations all over the place, wave the punkah for her guests, polish all her brasses . . . and she pays you next to nothing. I don't know how *you* stand it!

Messenger (*nodding*) Yes, sometimes she goes too far. You know she even wanted me to be her gatekeeper for this feast! But I persuaded her that I could get a couple of experts to do the job for what she thinks is a minimum price.

Serving Woman (*giggling*) Oh they do look a bit funny! And the little roly-poly one is sweet on me, just because I gave him a coconut *burfi* yesterday! Where on earth did you find such a pair?

Messenger (*grinning and tapping his nose*) That's for me to know.

Serving Woman Oh go on! *Batao na!*

Messenger (*nodding*) Okay, but you must keep it a secret. Promise?

Serving Woman My lips are sealed.

Messenger After their encounter with Ali Baba, the forty thieves went out of business. They scattered around the world looking for employment, but no one would hire them because all they could do was rob. I felt sorry for them, so I built an extension to my house and persuaded them to move in and go into business with me. It's the security business, and they've all become gatekeepers and bodyguards, and I'm their secret trainer and manager.

Serving Woman Oh my!

Messenger Training them was hard work, mind you! They had this fixed idea that everyone had to have the password 'Open Sesame!' before they'd be allowed in!

Serving Woman Oh my! But what do *you* get out of all this?

Messenger Well, I won't stay at her beck and call for ever. You must have noticed that Her Snobbiness demands the most fabulous presents from everyone who calls on her, and every present has to come through the gatekeepers. I've come to the decision that she certainly doesn't deserve all of those magnificent gifts; so, with the help of my two thieves, some of them are going to find a new home! We believe in equal shares for all.

Serving Woman You *are* clever! But you'll be in awful trouble if you're caught! Can I help? And can I have a share? Ple-ea-se!

Messenger We-e-ll, what could you do to help?

Serving Woman You and the forty thieves must need a housekeeper.

Messenger So we do. We'll be happy to have you join us. You can have an equal share of whatever we get. But I warn you, the forty thieves are a very untidy lot!

They shake hands.

Serving Woman (*giggling*) They'll all have to give me the password 'Open Sesame!' before *I* let them in.

Holding hands, they skip around the fountain. Serving Woman then exits, leaving Messenger to prepare the stage for the next scene.

Act Four

The guests are dressed in gorgeous satins, velvets and silks. The two gatekeepers look grand in their uniforms as they stand to attention outside the palace gates. A red carpet is rolled out in front of the gates.

Gatekeepers One and Two (*practising their greetings*) Salaam, O honoured guests. *Namasté* and welcome. Salaam, *salaam aléikum*. Alright, mate? *Guten morgen. Hola. How.* Hi there! *Bonjour. Kombaawa*, etc.

Enter Kobi Kabir in his usual simple cotton clothes and carrying some papers in his hand. He does a pirouette and skips up to the gate but is stopped by the Gatekeepers.

Gatekeepers *Aré*, you *badmaash*! Hey, you rascal! Where do you think you are going?

They grab him.

Kobi Kabir *Chhor do, mujhé*. Let me go. I've come for the party. I'm here for the Lady Sharifa Snobbyshowoff Shahzada's feast.

Gatekeeper One (*laughing*) Ho, ho! Silly fellow! The red carpet isn't for the likes of you! We'll be carpeted if we let *you* in! No, no, you can't go in. Off with you! Fancy trying to enter this palace!

Kobi Kabir Let me in, please let me in. *Mujhé under jane do*. I've come for the feast.

Gatekeeper Two (*laughing maliciously*) Ho, ho! Ha, ha! You *buddhu*, you *bévacoof*! What a fool you are! Don't

25

you know that this party is only for important people –
not for the likes of you! Just look at your simple clothes –
they are poor and stupid. Fancy trying to gatecrash a
party that's only for the super-rich!

Kobi Kabir But I've brought a present for the Lady
Sharifa Snobbyshowoff Shahzada. *Dékho* – (*showing the
poem on a piece of paper*) – it's my latest poem.

Gatekeeper One You *buddhu*, you *bévacoof*! You fool!
Other guests are bringing gold, diamonds and pearls,
while you – you bring some cheap paper! Pah!

*He tears Kobi Kabir's papers and both Gatekeepers
throw the bits of paper on his head and laugh at him.*

Kobi Kabir Why are you treating me like this? I only
came for the feast.

Gatekeeper Two *Aré*, we have our orders right from the
top, you *buddhu*, you *bévacoof*, you fool – from the
Lady Sharifa Snobbyshowoff Shahzada herself. *Ab nikal
jao!* Now off with you! If you are hungry, take yourself
to the back door and line up with the other beggars and
tramps. There will be plenty of leftovers when your
betters have finished their feasting.

*Kobi Kabir tries to enter through the gate, but the
Gatekeepers grab him by the collar and drag him out.
Kobi Kabir lifts up a hand as if in surrender and
seems to leave. Then he walks up to the audience
and addresses them.*

Kobi Kabir Never mind. But I *will* go to the party.
I have a sneaky plan that should get me inside that gate.
Just watch this! (*He performs a pirouette, then begins to
walk backwards towards the gate.*)

Kobi Kabir (*in a loud voice and with hand-waving when
he comes near the gate*) Goodbye. *Sayonara. Shalom.
Khuda Hafiz. Nomoshkar. Adios . . .*

The Gatekeepers jump to attention and give a smart salute.

Gatekeepers One and Two (*shouting in unison*)
Goodbye, sir!

Kobi Kabir disappears through the gate.

Gatekeeper One That guest left early, didn't he? With a bit of luck we might finish early tonight. So give me a five!

He holds out his palm and Gatekeeper Two slaps it in good humour. A moment later Messenger appears, dragging Kobi Kabir by the collar. The two Gatekeepers stand at attention and salute.

Messenger (*angrily to the Gatekeepers*) Now stay awake, you two! You just let this fellow past you when his poor clothes should have told you that Her Ladyship won't want him at the feast. Smarten up or we'll all lose our jobs!

Gatekeepers One and Two (*saluting*) *Achha sa'ab!* Yes, sir!

Messenger goes back in.

Gatekeeper One (*to Kobi Kabir*) So, it's you again! You fooled us with your goodbyes! Well, you won't catch us out again, I can tell you. So be off with you!

Gatekeeper Two *Jao! Nikal jao!*

Kobi Kabir (*walking up to the audience*) Well, that sneaky plan didn't work, but never mind, I *will* go to the party. I have an even sneakier plan this time. Just watch this.

Kobi Kabir performs a pirouette, then makes a run for the gate, but the Gatekeepers are watching and they start chasing him. He leads them a merry chase right around the stage and the audience. When they get back near the gate, Gatekeeper Two looks tired and out of breath. He flops down.

Gatekeeper Two (*to Gatekeeper One*) *Tum jao, uska peechhe karo! Mujhé thora aaram karné do.*

Gatekeeper One Right you are, gaffer! You have a rest while I chase him.

Gatekeeper One chases Kobi Kabir right round the stage and the audience. When they get back near the gate, Gatekeeper One looks tired and out of breath. He flops down.

(*tapping Gatekeeper Two on the shoulder*) My turn to rest now, I'm puffed out. It's your turn to chase him.

Gatekeeper Two gets up and chases Kobi Kabir around the stage.

Kobi Kabir (*next time round, he stops near Gatekeeper One and taps him on the shoulder*) My turn to rest now, I'm puffed out. It's your turn to chase him.

Gatekeeper One gets up and starts chasing Gatekeeper Two. As they chase each other around the audience, Kobi Kabir smiles and gives the audience a broad wink. He performs a pirouette and coolly skips in through the gate. A moment later Messenger appears again, dragging Kobi Kabir by the collar. The two Gatekeepers are still chasing each other.

Messenger (*angrily to the Gatekeepers*) Now stop playing catch-as-catch-can! You two idiots have just let this fellow get past you again! I might as well be doing this job myself.

Gatekeepers One and **Two** (*sheepishly saluting*) Sorry, sir! *Maaph kar do, sa'ab!* It won't happen again.

*Messenger leaves Kobi Kabir with them and goes
back in.*

Gatekeeper One You fooled us again! I've a good mind
to give you a good thrashing!

*The two Gatekeepers raise their hands and are about
to hit him.*

Kobi Kabir Stop, stop! It was all a test. I'm not really a
poor gatecrasher at all. The Lady Sharifa Snobbyshowoff
Shahzada had employed me to see if I could get past
your eagle eyes. And I must say that, between you and
Messenger, you're doing a great job of ensuring security
for today's feast. (*He gives them both a pat on the back.*)
I shall be happy to go in and recommend you both to
Her Ladyship for a big *baksheesh*.

Gatekeepers One *and* **Two** (*gratified*) Achha. Khoob
bhalo! (*to each other*) We'll be getting a big reward! Oo-
oo-ooh!

*Kobi Kabir enters again. But a minute later Messenger
brings him out.*

Messenger (*to Kobi Kabir*) You know, I almost admire
your persistence and want to reward you with entry to
the Shahzada Mahal. But it's more than my job's worth
to let you in. And believe me, if you saw what a snobby
business the whole feast is you wouldn't want to come.
Now go.

Kobi Kabir But . . .

Gatekeeper One No 'buts'. Off with you!

*The two Gatekeepers give Kobi Kabir a little push in
the direction of the audience.*

Messenger (*turning to the Gatekeepers*) As for you two,
you've had your last chance. If he gets in again, I will

volunteer you both to do all the washing-up after this jamboree is over!

Messenger goes inside.

Kobi Kabir (*to the audience*) Never mind. But I *will* go to the party. I still have my best and sneakiest plan of all. But for this plan to work I'll have to go home first and change, and write another poem, which will just give you enough time to collect your presents and change for the feast. So, I'll see you all in a little while. (*waving*) *Sayonara* and *Khuda Hafiz*.

Kobi Kabir pirouettes and skips off the stage.

Act Five

The audience are now guests, who arrive in rich costumes and are carrying presents. They are dressed in gorgeous satins, velvets and silks. Some have long flowing trains that have to be held up by pages, some are wearing embroidered nagra slippers with great toe-curls at the front, some have pages holding up richly decorated parasols above their heads and some are wearing enormous turbans that sport gleaming jewels and long exotic feathers. The two Gatekeepers and Messenger welcome and usher in the guests, who all line up to step on the red carpet and enter through the gate. Messenger shows them to their seats.

Enter Kobi Kabir, now grandly dressed, but with dark glasses covering his eyes. The poet is wearing a very costly robe, turban, shoes and jewellery. He looks like an Eastern prince. His sword, in an elaborate scabbard, dangles from his belt and is so long that it trails behind him on the floor.

Gatekeeper Two (*to Gatekeeper One*) Aré, this must be some great *raj kumar*, a prince. Or maybe he is even a king or a *shahinshah*, an emperor. Look how the jewels sparkle in his turban!

Gatekeeper One And what a heavy and magnificent sword he is wearing! But this great *badshah* is visiting us incognito. Look – the dark glasses mean that he doesn't want to be recognised. But of course the Lady Sharifa Snobbyshowoff Shahzada is sure to know him – she knows everyone who is truly rich and important. Won't she just be tickled pink to see him!

As Kobi Kabir approaches the gate, the two
Gatekeepers rush to serve him.

Gatekeepers (*bowing*) A thousand salaams, O most
honoured guest. (*with palms joined*) *Namasté* and
welcome. *Swagatam. Ahalan wa sahalan. Salaam*
aléikum.

Gatekeeper One (*bowing*) *Kombawa*, O most honoured
guest. May I request your name and your present?

Kobi Kabir *Jaci da.* I am the Bounteous Badshah of
Bardford and mine is a very special present.

He takes out a scroll from a voluminous pocket in his
robe. It is rolled up and tied with a gold ribbon.
Gatekeeper Two reaches for it, but Kobi Kabir stops
him from taking it.

No, good fellows. I won't have you taking my present in
for my hostess, the Lady Sharifa Snobbyshowoff Shahzada.
It's a surprise and I mean to deliver it to her myself.

The Gatekeepers look at each other, confused.

Theek hai. It's okay, fellows. I know you have your
orders, but perhaps you do not know that the Lady
Sharifa Snobbyshowoff Shahzada, who adores receiving
presents, loves surprise presents most of all.

Gatekeepers (*bowing*) A thousand pardons, Your Most
Excellent Highness. We did not know. Forgive us and
please be gracious enough to enter this poor palace.

Kobi Kabir (*turns to face the audience, lifts his dark*
glasses a little, smiles and winks) Guess who's going to
the feast?

Then he enters through the gate, his long sword
clattering on the floor behind him. He takes his seat
with the rest of the guests.

Gatekeeper One Cor! I've never seen a prince more grand or more lordly. And what do you suppose his surprise present is?

Gatekeeper Two That paper must be the deed to some country or even an empire; it must be worth a *pukka* fortune! I wouldn't half like to watch milady's face when she gets that surprise present! This place – Bardford – must be a wonderfully exotic place to have a *badshah* like that!

Gatekeeper One Yeah. I must look it up in my atlas next time I get a chance. I might go there for my Eid holidays. I'll bring you back some of their *mitthai* if I do.

Gatekeeper Two (*licking his lips*) Mmm . . . How good of you! I too might go there for my Diwali holidays and see how they light up the place. I'll bring you some *mishti* too. Now let's see: there's *roshogollas* and *jilebees*, *chom choms* and *halwa*, pastry and . . .

Gatekeeper One You fool, didn't we agree not to talk about food?

Gatekeeper Two You're the one who started it!

Hits him on the head. Gatekeeper One hits him back. Then they start chasing each other and run offstage.

Kobi Kabir (*turns to face the audience*) Well, I got in. Do you think anyone recognised me in my disguise? I must say you all look magnificent. Her Snobby Ladyship will be very impressed. And, my friends, *mes amis, méré yaron, amar bondhura*, what wonderful presents you have all brought for Her Grasping Ladyship. But where is she? It would appear that the Lady Sharifa Snobby-showoff Shahzada intends to keep us waiting. That's good, *amigos mios*, because I have a little plan that will need your help.

He explains a signal to some of the guests so that they will later vomit on cue over the presents.

But not yet – wait for my signal. I wonder, where is Her Snobbiness? Let's see.

Act Six

*In the marbled cool of the Shahzada Mahal, Lady Sharifa
Snobbyshowoff Shahzada sits and has her toenails
painted by the serving woman. From time to time she
sips sherbet from a crystal goblet. Gentle sitar music is
in the background.*

Lady Sharifa Snobbyshowoff Shahzada *Jao*, go, take a
peek and tell me if the hall is full of my guests?

Serving Woman (*looking at the audience*) Oh yes, Your
Magnificence, it's quite full. There are people here from
many lands: princes and nobles, all the rich VIPs in their
gorgeous clothes. (*hurriedly*) But of course none are as
rich and as beautiful as you, Your Pomposity.

Lady Sharifa Snobbyshowoff Shahzada *Achha*, so my
messenger has done a good job of inviting people. And
have they all brought me nice presents?

Serving Woman Oh most excellent ones, *Begum Sahiba*!
They are all very costly and most worthy gifts, Your
Eminence.

Lady Sharifa Snobbyshowoff Shahzada (*clapping her
hands*) *Shabaash*! Goody! That's what I like to hear! And
are the jugglers, the dancers and the musicians waiting to
entertain them? Is my palace looking even more
wonderful than usual?

Serving Woman *Jee, Begum Sahiba*, all is in readiness.
The Shahzada Mahal is breathtakingly beautiful. Your
nails too are done now. The *mehndi* on your hands is

also long dry, Your Supreme Presence. So wouldn't you like to join your guests and begin the feast?

Lady Sharifa Snobbyshowoff Shahzada (*irritated*) Certainly not, you silly peasant! You should know by now that people like me always keep other people waiting – it shows how important I am. They must all be in suspense, waiting for me. Then, and only then, shall I make my grand entrance. No, no, I don't think they have waited enough. My importance requires that they wait some more. Any more such stupid suggestions from you and I will dismiss you from my service. Now go and warm the food.

Serving Woman Of course, Your High and Mightiness. (*to the audience*) It's a good job I've got an opening with Messenger and the forty thieves! I'm not at all frightened now of the Snobby She-Monster. She can do her worst! What do I care? In fact I might just hand in my notice, but I must pick the right moment for it.

Serving Woman exits and Messenger enters.

Messenger *Suno, suno*, Your Ladyship!

Lady Sharifa Snobbyshowoff Shahzada What now? Can't you see I'm relaxing?

Messenger A mystery guest has arrived. He is magnificently rich and comes bearing a surprise present for you. He is the bountiful and bounteous Badshah of Bardford. He is already at the feast.

Lady Sharifa Snobbyshowoff Shahzada What? And I am sitting here. You *bevacoof*, you fool, I should have been there to receive him. Take me to the feast immediately and announce my presence.

Messenger Of course, *Begum Sahiba*!

Act Seven

*Inside the magnificent Shahzada Mahal there are guests
(the children from the audience) who are milling around
and talking. In one corner of the room is a large pile of
presents. A European juggler-jester dressed in bells and
motley is juggling his way through the audience. There is
Indian music in the background, quite slow to start with,
but the tempo increases. Suddenly Messenger enters and
there is a drum roll. The music stops and everyone
stands still and looks at Messenger, who jingles his
anklets and shakes his dumaru for a moment.*

Messenger Hear ye, hear ye. *Suno, suno.* Ladies and
gentlemen of Kahanistan, *Kahanistan ké shrimaan-
shrimati, khawateen-o-hazraat. Attention, attention, s'il
vous plaît!* You there, attention please! Be upstanding for
our hostess, the beautiful Lady Sharifa Snobbyshowoff
Shahzada!

She is just about to enter and curtsy when . . .

Kobi Kabir Sit down! Now let's have some music and
dance.

*Music starts again and Kobi Kabir, Messenger and
Serving Woman dance an Indian classical dance. Lady
Sharifa Snobbyshowoff Shahzada watches and tries to
join in but gets a bit confused as the music turns into
Bollywood cinema music and then into European
disco and then abruptly stops.*

Messenger Ladies and gentlemen of Kahanistan,
Kahanistan ké khawateen-o-hazraat, shrimaan-shrimati!

Your attention, *s'il vous plaît*! (*Gestures to the audience/
guests to stand up.*) Be upstanding for our hostess, the
beautiful Lady Sharifa Snobbyshowoff Shahzada!

Kobi Kabir No, no, sit down! I'd much rather dance!

> *Music starts again and they all do a vigorous bhangra-
> type dance during which Messenger dances off the
> stage, and at the end . . .*

Lady Sharifa Snobbyshowoff Shahzada (*rushing up to
Kobi Kabir, smiling and curtsying*) Welcome, welcome,
Your Magnificent Highness. *Namasté* and *salaam
aléikum.*

> *She claps her hands and Serving Woman rushes in
> with a flower garland, which she hands Her Ladyship
> who, in her turn, puts it over Kobi Kabir.*

I am absolutely thrilled that you have come to my
humble little palace and my most unworthy feast. Please
come and sit at my right hand, on my special cushion.

> *Kobi Kabir follows her with a flourish. After he and
> his hostess are seated, the rest of the guests and the
> audience sit down too.*

Lady Sharifa Snobbyshowoff Shahzada (*simpering*) I am
told that you have a wonderful surprise present for me –
I wonder what it could be! Perhaps it's the Golden
Goblet of Greece or the Radiant Red Ruby of Rajasthan.
I do so love surprise presents. (*She holds out a hand.*)
So may I . . . ?

Kobi Kabir You have grasped the matter rightly but,
Your Grasping Ladyship, it is a surprise that must wait
till the end of the feast. If you see it now, it won't be a
surprise at the right time. (*He does a piroutte and then
sings.*)

A word to the wise:
What is a surprise?
A beggar in disguise
Or a king telling lies?
If you see it with your eyes,
The element of surprise
Surely dies, surely dies.

He does a piroutte again. The Lady Sharifa Snobby-showoff Shahzada and all her guests clap.

Lady Sharifa Snobbyshowoff Shahzada *Bohot achha*, very well, I am sure you know best, Your Extraordinary Excellence! (*clapping her hands for her Serving Woman*) Fetch the punkah wallah for our honoured guest's comfort.

Serving Woman grabs a couple of presents from the pile as she leaves the stage. Messenger dances in. He is carrying a large fan of peacock feathers for he is also the Lady Sharifa Snobbyshowoff Shahzada's punkah wallah. He positions himself behind Kobi Kabir and proceeds to fan him. Kobi Kabir removes his garland and also pulls out his ribboned scroll and hands these to Messenger for safe-keeping.

Kobi Kabir My fine fellow, I know I can trust you to look after this present until after the feast is ended.

Messenger bows and takes the present. Then he picks up a crystal glass and tinkles on it with a spoon to draw the attention of all the guests.

Lady Sharifa Snobbyshowoff Shahzada Ladies and gentlemen of Kahanistan, *Kahanistan ké khawateen-o-hazraat, shrimaan-shrimati*! Let the feast begin. (*turning to Kobi Kabir*) Your Greatest Eminence, I would greatly value your esteemed opinion on each one of my exquisite dishes. First the *hors d'oeuvres* – we have a range of starters to select from. Let me offer you my prized *pappadoms*. No ordinary *pappadoms*, these. They are coated with *kala mirch*, they're peppered *pappadoms* from Purulia in Assam.

She claps her hands and Serving Woman brings in a platter piled high with pappadoms.

Here, let me personally serve Your Honourable Magniloquence.

She takes the platter from Serving Woman's hands and dismisses her with a gesture. Messenger takes the opportunity to garland Serving Woman with the welcoming garland. Again, as Serving Woman leaves, she helps herself to a present from the corner of the room.

Kobi Kabir (*nods approvingly*) *Achha, pappadoms* with *kala mirch*. Always a great beginning to any feast.

He picks up some pappadoms *and crumbles them in his hands. Then he sprinkles the crumbs on himself. The Lady Sharifa Snobbyshowoff Shahzada looks very puzzled and the guests start whispering among themselves.*
    Lady Sharifa Snobbyshowoff Shahzada hurriedly claps her hands and Serving Woman brings in a platter piled high with pakoras *and a bowl of sauce.*

Lady Sharifa Snobbyshowoff Shahzada Perhaps Your Grandiose Benevolence is not partial to pepper, but won't you try some of these aubergine *pakoras*, dipped in a delicate mint-and-coriander sauce? They are the speciality of my Punjabi head cook, the celebrated Pankaj Puri.

Kobi Kabir *Achha*, I'm always ready for *pakoras*, and aubergine *pakoras* are my favourites.

He picks up two round pakoras, *throws them up in the air, catches them and squashes them on his head.*

Kobi Kabir Now, didn't you say something about a delicate mint-and-coriander sauce to accompany the *pakoras*?

He carefully spoons the sauce onto his shoes. Then he takes out a large and beautiful handkerchief and proceeds to polish both his shoes with it. The Lady Sharifa Snobbyshowoff Shahzada looks very worried and the guests gasp at his unusual behaviour.

Yes, the sauce was a treat alright – my shoes took a right shine to them! My compliments to the celebrated Pankaj Puri of the Punjab.

Lady Sharifa Snobbyshowoff Shahzada hurriedly claps her hand and Serving Woman brings in tray after tray holding various dishes. Each time she leaves the stage she takes another present with her. Her Ladyship is nervous, so she gabbles on:

Lady Sharifa Snobbyshowoff Shahzada Perhaps Your Bountifulness would care for some *gobi ka paratha* or some *naan* bread, or maybe an Italian pizza with a cheese, olive and anchovy topping? Or there's spaghetti Bolognese too, cooked to perfection by my Italian chef, Signor Salvatore Silvano, and on these plates the softest white *idlis* and finest *dhosas* from South India. Or what about some pilau rice – I get only the best basmati, mind you, cooked in the purest ghee; it is coated with rare saffrons from the valleys of Kashmir, and embellished with almonds, raisins and cardamoms. And it goes ever so well with all these curries: there's a vegetable curry here with *bhindi*, ladies fingers, *tinda* and pumpkin. And here are a chicken *vindaloo* with potatoes and a *saag-gost*, spinach with lamb meat. My chef, Ustad Haroon

Khan from Pak Pathaan in Pakistan, cooks a scrumptious
tikka masala. And I hope you like fish because my Bengali
chef, Monmohon Mishti Miah, is a master at cooking
fish curries: there's *rui maach* cooked in yoghurt, and
ilish maach garnished with chillies and *koi maach* so
fresh that the *koi* almost leap into your mouth. As for
this salad, my Japanese chef, Michiko, is quite an artist
in the way that she cuts the vegetables and fruits; she
arranges them so tastefully, too. I am sure there must be
something here to tempt you and to tickle your taste
buds. Please choose whatever you would like.

Kobi Kabir *Achha, achha*, it's quite a feast you've spread
here. I must certainly do it justice. These strings of
Italian spaghetti will be nice extensions dangling from
my earrings. (*He drapes some spaghetti behind his ears.*)
What do you think? Would Signor Salvatore Silvano
approve? I might even be able to wear the spaghetti
hoops on my fingers as rings. (*He flashes his ringed
fingers.*) As for this *naan* bread, it will fit nicely in my
breast pocket. (*He picks up the* naan, *tears it in half and
shoves it in his breast pocket.*) The *idli* will be snug in
another pocket and of course I mustn't forget the *dhosa*!
(*He deposits these in other pockets.*) The pizza with all
its wonderful toppings must of course top my head. I'm
without a mirror at the moment, Your Dementedness, so
please check if I've placed it correctly on the top of my
silk *pagree*.

> *The Lady Sharifa Snobbyshowoff Shahzada looks
> horrified now and all the guests are smothering their
> laughter and are muttering. One of them has a
> demented snorting laugh. None of them are eating now.*

Lady Sharifa Snobbyshowoff Shahzada (*weakly*) The
pizza – ye-es. But I thought you would appreciate the
food. I don't understand – I don't understand any of this!

Kobi Kabir Oh, but there are so many more goodies here. Let's see now. This fish curry by Monmohon Mishti Miah will slide nicely down my left sleeve, and the tomato chutney will look ever so colourful down my right sleeve. And let me take a look at these drinks. *Lassi* with just a hint of rosewater – that can decorate the left leg of my trousers and give it a delicate perfume. As for the right leg, it really must enjoy this delightful watermelon sherbet. I wonder if this kebab will look stylish next to the feather in my *pagree*? Well, there's nothing for it but to try it and see, especially if it's cooked by the famous Ustad Haroon Khan from Pak Pathaan in Pakistan. Now these sticky *jilebees* – I'll stick them in my belt. These chips will go in so – one in each ear.

He carefully pours rice pudding on his robe. Three soft white roshagollas *are pushed into the folds of his turban.*

Lady Sharifa Snobbyshowoff Shahzada How dare you insult me like this! Are you making fun of my food?

Kobi Kabir I'm so sorry, Your Atrocious Majesty, but I can't hear a word you are saying! With these chips in my ears, my hearing has had its chips. Do excuse me, I must get on with all the piles of food that still remain. Some of the colours rather clash with my clothes, but I'm not fussy. This delicious carrot *halwa* – let me spread it all over the front of my *uchhkin*. This *masoor dal* has a lovely fragrance and a nice smooth consistency to it – I think I'll just pour it down my back. As for these celery sticks – I think I'll shove them up my nostrils.

Lady Sharifa Snobbyshowoff Shahzada Stop it, stop it! You – you *paagal*, you madman! How dare you?

Kobi Kabir (*to the audience*) Aha, I think I'm finally getting to her. (*to Her Ladyship*) Dearest Looniness, don't get your knickers in such a twist while I'm trying to do full justice to every food item here. Ah, baked beans! *Yeh khana mujhe bohot pasand hain!* They are a favourite – and this looks suitably runny. I'll let it make a nice splash or two as I pour it on my buttons.

Kobi gives a signal for some of the guests to be sick over the presents.

Lady Sharifa Snobbyshowoff Shahzada (*to Kobi Kabir*) *Baap ré baap!* You are – you are a complete *paagal*! You're certainly mad, loony, crazy, off your head, round the bend. You have completely spoilt my feast and are driving me insane.

Messenger (*helpfully*) Your Monstrosity, with the chips decorating his ears, not to mention all the strings of Italian spaghetti, the Bountiful Badshah of Bardford can't hear you.

Lady Sharifa Snobbyshowoff Shahzada Oh! (*Removes the chips from Kobi Kabir's ears, then looks at her soiled fingers distastefully.*) Now look what you've made me do! My beautiful hands are all dirty with your chips!

Kobi Kabir (*innocently*) Surely not! I didn't think you would be serving dirty food to all your guests!

Kobi gives a signal for more guests to throw up over the presents.

Lady Sharifa Snobbyshowoff Shahzada Stop it! You – all of you – you are driving me bananas with all your lunatic antics.

Serving Woman quickly hands her mistress a bunch of bananas. Her Ladyship tears them one by one and throws them at her ducking and grinning maid. As a result of Serving Woman's ducking, the bananas hit some of the guests.

Oh, you have humiliated me in front of all my guests.
I want you to leave. *Nikal jao!* Get out! Get out!

Kobi Kabir (*innocently*) *Achha?* Your Supreme Snobbiness, it seems that you've really had enough humiliation?
But before I leave, don't you want your surprise present?

Lady Sharifa Snobbyshowoff Shahzada (*confused*)
Present? Oh yes, of course, *méri tofa*, my present, where
is it? What is it? *Mujhé jaldi dé do.* Quickly, give it to me.

> *Messenger carefully presents Kobi Kabir with the
> ribboned scroll, which is now resting on a velvet
> cushion.*

Kobi Kabir Here it is, a most magnificent gift.

> *All the guests crowd to see it. Her Ladyship is about
> to grab it when he slaps her hand.*

Not so fast. I wonder if you have ever had anyone write
a poem to you before?

Lady Sharifa Snobbyshowoff Shahzada (*haughtily*) Oh
bohot dafa! Many times! Men are always sending me
poems and singing me songs about my great beauty: my
honey-coloured eyes, which are sweet as syrup, my long
hair which flows like the Ganges, my figure, which is like
that of *apsaras, houris* and angels, and of course my face,
which is just like a lotus in full bloom!

Kobi Kabir *Achha*, that may well be, but no one has as
yet written in praise of your wealth, have they? And
surely that is a worthy subject for poetry?

Lady Sharifa Snobbyshowoff Shahzada No, I haven't
had such a poem before. *Achha*, recite the poem before
you go.

Kobi Kabir (*to all the guests and the audience*) You can
all join in with me by repeating Her Ladyship's name

45

whenever I recite it, and (*to Her Ladyship*) your name of course figures quite a lot in my poem.

Lady Sharifa Snobbyshowoff Shahzada And quite right too! It is a bea-u-ti-ful name!

Kobi Kabir A foolish lady's gold was popular,
　　Sharifa Snobbyshowoff Shahzada.

The audience repeat this line.

Poor Kobi Kabir was not to be fed,
Only his well-heeled shoes and clothes instead.
Many came to her palace to woo her.
She was a show-off – that didn't put off
The many who 'loved' her for her treasure.
They would bow and they would curtsy, and doff
Their caps in pretended admiration.
What attracted their appreciation
Were goblets of gold and platters of silver,
Her diamonds and pearls, her crystal vases,
Her rubies, emeralds, all her riches.
These were what made the lady popular,
Sharifa Snobbyshowoff Shahzada.

The audience repeat this line.

Sharifa Snobbyshowoff Shahzada,

The audience repeat this line.

A foolish lady, to be popular
Would throw huge parties and only invite
The rich and the famous who did alright
And could give her very costly presents.
(The lady's pride and her greed represents
All that's nasty in pompous vanity.)
She had her diamonds but no sincere friend,
She invited a rich *badshah* to spend
Some time at her marble palace and feast

Because of his *nagra* shoes, his silk robes,
The golden turban on his haughty head.
Poor Kobi Kabir was not to be fed,
Only his well-heeled shoes and clothes instead.
A foolish lady's gold was popular,
Sharifa Snobbyshowoff Shahzada.

*The audience repeat this line. Kobi Kabir does a
piroutte.*

Lady Sharifa Snobbyshowoff Shahzada Oh you horrid
and dreadful man, you *badmaash*! Who on earth are
you?

Kobi Kabir (*removes his dark glasses with a flourish and
does another piroutte*) Poor Kobi Kabir, My Lady. The
Bard of Bardford. I am a great poet,

The Messenger provides a drum roll.

Ami moha kobi.

Drum roll.

I write all kinds of verse:

Flute notes.

nana chhora likhi:

Flute notes.

stories, poems, letters,

Sitar tune.

golpo, kabbo, chhiti,

Sitar tune.

I recite them all.

Shahnai note.

shob kori abritti.

47

Shahnai note.

There is such power in the pen!

Drum roll.

Kolomér achhé kee shokti!

Drum roll.

There is such power in the pen! But you thought that power was only in wealth. But there's power in so many other things in life – for instance in health, in goodness, in a good reputation.

Lady Sharifa Snobbyshowoff Shahzada (*in a rage*) Messenger, call the gatekeepers and have this – this beastly bard thrown out into the gutters! I never want to see or hear him again!

Messenger Thank you, *merci beaucoup, shukriya*, Kobi Kabir, for making this the happiest day I've enjoyed in a very long while! (*turning to face Her Ladyship*) As for you, My Lady Snobby She-Monster, find someone else to do your dirty work! I won't work for you any more.

Lady Sharifa Snobbyshowoff Shahzada (*spluttering*) What! What! (*to Serving Woman*) Serving Woman, fetch my gatekeepers at once! (*to Messenger*) I'll have them beat you black and blue, you *and* the poet. (*shaking her fist at them*) You'll both be sorry you ever crossed my path.

Serving Woman I'm out of here too! I should have done this a long time ago. I'll no longer slave away for a wicked, mean and snobby show-off like you! Besides, the gatekeepers won't take any notice of you. They work for Messenger. So, if you give them stupid orders about him, they might end up beating you instead! (*to Messenger*) Come, I've got our presents hidden away; let's collect them and quit this miserable place.

*A smiling Messenger, Serving Woman and the guests
dance a happy and boisterous goodbye conga around
the stage. Messenger waves a colourful hanky at the
audience and Serving Woman blows kisses as they
leave. Kobi Kabir waves farewell to them and
encourages the audience also to wave goodbye.*

Lady Sharifa Snobbyshowoff Shahzada Good grief! The
whole world's gone mad! And it's all because of you –
(*looking daggers at Kobi Kabir*) – you – you *shair*, you
kobi, you poet! You have deliberately insulted me! You
waste my food, throwing it all over your clothes. You
have not tasted any of these magnificent dishes that are
fit for a king. You haven't had anything to drink. Well,
was my food not good enough for you?

Kobi Kabir (*smiling*) You now feel the anger I felt when
I was first turned away at your gate. The gatekeepers'
orders came from you, so it was you who insulted and
humiliated me. It's not a question of your food not being
good enough for me – it was clearly I who, in your
opinion, was not good enough for *your* food. Your
gatekeepers mocked me and barred me from entering the
Shahzada Mahal, they tore up my poems and threw me
out because I wore simple ordinary clothes. But later
I came in these costly robes that I won in a poetry
competition held to find the Bard of Bardford – I never
wore them until now. And when you saw me in these
clothes, you rushed to welcome me and treated me like
a most honoured guest. It seems that your invitation to
this wonderful feast was not for me, but for my clothes.
So it's only fair that all this delicious food and drink
should be given to my clothes!

Lady Sharifa Snobbyshowoff Shahzada (*hitting Kobi
Kabir with a cucumber which she has picked up from
a plate*) Oh! And to think that I curtsied to you, you

battameez! You beast! I really thought you were the Badshah of Bardford! I'll have you kicked, I'll have you flogged and tortured! No one will ever invite you again! I'll . . .

Kobi Kabir But no one will ever *accept* another invitation from *you* again in this land. Everyone now knows you for the snobby and mean show-off that you are! All your guests will now spread the word. You are a laughing stock! No longer will people flatter you or bring you costly presents.

Lady Sharifa Snobbyshowoff Shahzada *Meri tofa!* At least I still have my wonderful presents from this evening!

She rushes to the corner, where only a few presents remain and grabs these in her arms. But she recoils too late when she realises that the presents are covered in vomit.

EEK! AARGH! You horrid man! And those horrible smelly guests – they did this! All my lovely presents covered in yuk! (*She leaves the stage shrieking and wailing.*)

Kobi Kabir (*standing alone on the stage and facing the audience*) I didn't get to eat or drink anything, but you know what? I must say that I've enjoyed feasting my eyes and ears on all that went on at the feast in the Shahzada Mahal. Perhaps if the Lady Sharifa Snobbyshowoff Shahzada had only been kinder and more friendly to other people, none of this would have happened. As it is, I think that her servants have only taken what is due to them and she herself has got her just deserts! (*Chuckles*) Her just desserts! (*He does a pirouette.*) But what do *you* think?

Curtain falls.

Author's Note

The Honoured Guest is a multicultural and multilingual play that is also a joyous celebration of food, language and culture. It offers an exciting adaptation of a traditional folk tale from the Indian subcontinent; its charm and humour carry an important didactic message for young children everywhere. The rich layers of this play allow scope for considerable discussion of issues pertaining to hospitality, cultural differences, power, fame, flattery, modesty, talent, skills, worth, wealth and sharing.

This is a playful play in which poetry, wordplay and alliteration abound. Words are explored for sound as well as meaning, and the vocabulary and understanding of a young audience are gently stretched. Language, principally poetry, is the dominant art form – the hero is a traditional bard and his name, Kobi, is also the Bengali word for poet (*kavi* in Hindi and Sanskrit). *Kabir* is the Arabic word for great and was also the name of a celebrated Muslim weaver-saint and Hindi poet of fifteenth-century India.

Although language is most important in this exuberant and interactive play, it is also a convergence of many art forms: dance, song, music, puppetry, clowning and mask-making, to name but a few. The dances range from classical to modern and include the ancient and highly theatrical Kathakali dance from South India and the modern and hilarious conga from the West. It is also a highly visual play in which vivid colours and costumes contribute a most important dimension.

Humour in the play operates at many levels, from elementary slapstick clowning to situational humour, as well as through a more sophisticated verbal humour employing puns and alliteration. It is a play that will, therefore, repay rereading and more than one viewing.

Naturally the multilingual nature of the play and the repetitive quality of much of the language allow considerable scope for easy language learning to take place, both in English and in other languages. The meanings of non-English words and phrases are generally understood from the context of the play; but a Glossary follows, which should be helpful in this respect. The main non-English languages used in the play are Bengali, Hindi and Urdu; but there are also words and phrases from , various other languages, including Arabic, French, Spanish, Italian, Hebrew, Japanese and Welsh. The many connections between languages, especially those belonging within linguistic families such as the Indo-European, will be readily apparent and should aid in language retention.

The Honoured Guest also contains many references that will be helpful in other educational subject areas such as History, Geography and – most obviously – Cookery. A few ideas for children's projects are given below.

A very simple version of the traditional tale upon which this play is based, may be found in the bilingual anthology *The Snake Prince and Other Folk Tales from Bengal*, edited by Debjani Chatterjee and Rehana Choudhury, and published in 1999 by BWSG Book Project, 11 Donnington Road, Sheffield S2 2RF at £7.99 (ISBN 0–95198–214–1).

Project Work

Note that these suggestions will involve some research and they may be better done in pairs or even in small groups with each child helping the others. Children should be encouraged to consult picture encyclopedias and dictionaries.

1   Do a project on 'Dances from Around the World'. Keep a scrapbook of pictures and photographs to illustrate different types of dances. Learn a few basic steps of any classical Indian dance and ballet.

2   Do a project on costumes from around the world. Keep a scrapbook of pictures and photographs to illustrate different types of costumes. Learn how to wear a sari or tie a *pagree* (turban).

3   Do a project on languages from around the world. On a map of the world, using a different colour for each language, identify where five different languages are spoken. Either learn how to count to ten in three different languages, or learn to say *please* and *thank you* in five different languages. Learn a nursery rhyme in any South Asian language.

4   Do a project on food and drink from around the world. Keep a scrapbook of pictures and photographs to illustrate different types of food. Learn how to make vegetable samosas and mix a good *lassi* or *ghol* – both the savoury and the sweet kinds. Learn about the importance of food presentation and try to prepare a salad that involves cutting various items in

fancy shapes: e.g., tomatoes shaped as flowers and cucumber sliced in star shapes. Learn about avoiding salmonella and food poisoning.

5　Do a project on musical instruments from around the world. Keep a scrapbook of pictures and photographs to illustrate different types of instruments. Learn to sing a song in a South Asian language and try to add some musical accompaniment.

6　Do a project on countries around the world. Use a good atlas to look up the different countries and places that are mentioned in the play (though Bardford of course is an imaginary place). List the capital city and the spoken language of each country that is mentioned.

7　Do a project on palaces from around the world. Keep a scrapbook of pictures and photographs of different palaces. Learn about the Great Moghuls and in particular about Shahjahan the Magnificent. Do your own drawing of what the Shahzada Mahal might look like with its marble pillars 'carved with exotic trees and fantastic flowers and birds'.

8　Retell the story of *The Honoured Guest* and include your own favourite food dishes in your version of the story. Try to retell any other traditional tales involving food: e.g., the story of the Gingerbread Man, and of Krishna in childhood stealing butter. Can you think of any other traditional stories in which there are little rhymes (e.g., 'Fee fi fo fum, I smell the blood of an Englishman!' in the story of *Jack and the Beanstalk*)? See if you can find any Indian stories about the legendary Maharaja Vikramaditya who had nine 'jewels' at his court.

9　Do a project on different ways of welcoming honoured guests. Write a letter to the Lord Mayor of Bardford, inviting him or her to visit your school for some occasion. In the letter, mention the different ways in which you will welcome the Lord Mayor. Learn about such customs as 'rolling out the red carpet', showering rose petals (compare this with showering confetti), drawing *rangoli* or *alpona* designs on the floor and garlanding a guest. Draw your own *rangoli* or *alpona* design on paper.

Glossary

CHARACTERS

Salwar-kameez A tunic-and-trouser set worn by women in northern India and Pakistan.

Sharifa Sharif is an Arabic word for 'noble' and *Sharifa* means a noble lady.

Shahzada A Persian word for a princely ruler.

Kathakali A classical dance from South India. Kathakali dancers wear very full skirts and very striking make-up, including a large artificial beard.

Dumaru A tiny Indian hand-held drum. Nataraja, the Lord of the Dance, is shown in Indian iconography as carrying a *dumaru* in one hand whose drum beat gives him the rhythm for his dance as well as the rhythm of the universe.

Punkah wallah A servant in the subcontinent whose task is to keep people cool by fanning them with a *punkah*, or fan. Electric fans and airconditioners have now made the punkah wallah's job redundant.

Tika A decorative marking on the forehead, usually in red.

ACT ONE

Mes amis My friends (*French*).

Méré yaron My friends (*Hindi/Urdu*).

Amar bondhura My friends (*Bengali*).

Namasté Greetings. Also *Namaskar* (*Hindi*). This greeting is accompanied by the palms joined together and the head bowed.

Salaam aléikum Muslim greeting, literally meaning 'Peace be upon you' (*Arabic*). It is accompanied by lifting the palm to the heart and to the forehead. The customary reply is *Walekum assalaam* (*Arabic*).

Bonjour Greetings. Literally 'Good day' (*French*). This is often accompanied by a kiss on both cheeks.

Kombaawa Greetings (*Japanese*).This is accompanied by a bow.

Hola Greetings (*Spanish*).

Ciao Greetings (*Italian*).

Ghudyambo Greetings (*Swahili*).This is accompanied by lifting up the palms.

Top of the morning to you Greetings (*Irish*).

Kahanistan The Land of Stories (*Hindi/Urdu*).

Jewel at the Court of Maharaja Vikramaditya
 Vikramaditya was a legendary king of Ujjain, in India, about whom many stories are told. He was said to have nine of the wisest and most learned men at his court; they were called the Jewels of his Court and included the celebrated Sanskrit poet-playwright Kalidas. A maharaja is a great raja or king.

Achha Okay (*Hindi/Urdu*).

Ami moha kobi I am a great poet (*Bengali*).

Nana chhora likhi I write all kinds of verse (*Bengali*).

Golpo, kabbo, chhiti Stories, poems, letters (*Bengali*).

Shahnai An Indian musical instrument with a plaintive sound, often played at weddings (*Hindi/Urdu/Bengali*).

Shob kori abritti I recite them all (*Bengali*).

Kolomér achhé kee shokti There is such power in the pen (*Bengali*).

Dékho Look (*Hindi/Urdu*). The same word is *dakho* in Bengali.

Daén dékho Look to the right (*Hindi/Urdu*).

Baén dékho Look to the left (*Hindi/Urdu*).

Kya yéh kahani such hai? Is this a true story? (*Hindi/Urdu*).

Ei golpo ki shotthi? Is this a true story? (*Bengali*).

Suno Listen (*Hindi/Urdu*). The same word is *shono* in Bengali.

Kahanistan ké shrimaan-shrimati Ladies and gentlemen of Kahanistan (*Hindi*).

Khawateen-o-hazraat Ladies and gentlemen (*Urdu*).

Attention, attention, s'il vous plaît Attention please (*French*).

Kal Tomorrow (*Hindi/Urdu*).

Kaalké Tomorrow (*Bengali*).

Bokra Tomorrow (*Arabic*).

Demain Tomorrow (*French*).

Shabaash Well done (*Hindi/Urdu/Bengali*).

Bravo Well done (*French*, but has come into English usage).

Mahal Palace (*Hindi/Urdu*).

Taj Mahal A marble mausoleum built by the Mughal emperor Shahjahan in honour of his empress Mumtaz Mahal. It is one of the wonders of the world.

Rangoli, alpona Designs drawn on the floor to welcome guests in India.

Jaldi batao Quickly tell (*Hindi/Urdu*).

Adios amigos Goodbye, friends (*Spanish*).

Au revoir Goodbye (*French*).

Khoob dhoni aar bishishto loke Very rich and important people (*Bengali*).

Taj Mahal jaisa sundar As beautiful as the Taj Mahal (*Hindi/Urdu*).

Hai Alas (*Hindi/Urdu/Bengali*).

Mai ék nazm – ék kavita – likhunga I will write a poem (*Hindi/Urdu*). The word for 'poem' is *nazm* in Urdu and *kavita* in Hindi.

Ami aik kobita likhbo I will write a poem (*Bengali*).

Hai na? Isn't that so? (*Hindi/Urdu*).

ACT TWO

Aur yéh bhi dékho And see this too (*Hindi/Urdu*).

Lekin yéh do buddhu kya kar rahé hai? But what are these two idiots up to? (*Hindi/Urdu*).

Pulaoér pahar A mountain of pulao rice (*Bengali*).

Biryanir bahar A splendour of biryani (*Bengali*).

Khathaaler jhol Jackfruit curry (*Bengali*).

Golapi gondhé ghol Buttermilk perfumed with rose fragrance (*Bengali*).

Aloo bhaja Fried potatoes (*Bengali*).

Doi bora A dish of ground lentil cakes in yoghurt (*Bengali*).

Laoo kumro Gourd and pumpkin (*Bengali*).

Machhér muro Fish head (*Bengali*). Bengalis consider the head of a fish to be a special treat for honoured guests.

Shag shobji Spinach and greens (*Bengali*).

Tatka chingri Fresh prawns (*Bengali*).

Mottoshuti phoolkopi Green peas and cauliflower (*Bengali*).

Roshogolla aar jilebee Roshogollas are white round sweets made from milk and in a sugary syrup. They are a Bengali speciality. *Jilebees* are fried sweets that are very sticky (*Bengali*).

Chom chom aar aloor dom Chom choms are sweets and *aloor dom* is a potato curry (*Bengali*).

Kee moja What fun (*Bengali*).

Halwa A sweet dish (*Bengali*).

Nishchoi Certainly (*Bengali*).

Ato joré chitkaar korbar kono dorkar nei, ami shob shunté parchhi There's no need to shout so loudly, I can hear everything (*Bengali*).

Tumi kee bollé? What did you say? (*Bengali*).

Na, na, motei na No, no, not at all (*Bengali*).

Ami to jege chhilam atokkhoo-oo-n dhore I've been awake all this time (*Bengali*).

Morpheus The Greek god of dreams.

Shundori Shrimoti Sharifa Snobbyshowoff Shahzada kee opurbo khabar khawabe othithhider What wonderful food the beauteous Lady Sharifa Snobbyshowoff Shahzada will be feeding her guests (*Bengali*).

Amritor moto khabar Food like nectar (*Bengali*).

Amra khabarer ak talika korte pari We could make a list of the food dishes (*Bengali*).

Eito tomar bhool That's your mistake (*Bengali*).

Shundori Shrimoti Sharifa Snobbyshowoff Shahzadar oti shundor aar doyalu jhee amay pochhondo koré The beauteous Lady Sharifa Snobbyshowoff Shahzada's extremely beautiful and kind maidservant fancies me (*Bengali*).

Shé amae boléchhé ki ki khabar to-uri koréchhé aar shé amadér jonno khabar tulé rékhéchhé She has told me of the different kinds of food she has prepared and she has saved some food for us (*Bengali*).

Theek bolecho You are correct (*Bengali*).

Aré hai Oh yes (*Bengali*).

Amra jé shob training *péyéchi, nana bhashae desh-bidesher othithhider shagot kora – sheshober ektu* practise *hoye jaak* All the training that we've received in greeting and welcoming guests from many lands – let's practise some of it (*Bengali*).

Kee bolo? What do you say? (*Bengali*).

Na, na, khobordar na! Éta ami bhebechi, tai ami tomai proshno korbo! Ami tomar porikkha nebo No, no, never. I thought of it, so I'll be the one to question you. I'll be the one to test you (*Bengali*).

Ami I (*Bengali*).

Achha, achha! Onik hoyeche Okay, okay! That's enough (*Bengali*).

Thhamo ebar Now stop (*Bengali*).

Theek achhe, tumi amar porikkha nebe aar ami tomar.
  Kamon? Okay, I'll test you and you'll test me.
  Alright? (*Bengali*).
Achha, Baba, achha Oh alright, alright (*Bengali*).
Amra dujonei porikkha nebo, kintu ami agé We'll both
  test each other, but I'll be the first one (*Bengali*).
Na, na, prothomé apni No, no, you first (*Bengali*).
Olé, olé Bravo (*Spanish*).
How Amerindian greeting, accompanied by a raised
  hand with palm facing the person greeted.
Ami kee koré ta janbo? Motéi Red Indian dakhachhé na
  How should I know that? You certainly don't look
  like a Red Indian (*Bengali*).
haka A spectacular Maori greeting from New Zealand,
  it is traditionally performed by Maori warriors and
  looks quite fierce (*Maori*).
Me old mucker My old mate (English colloquial).
Aré, bokaram! Amai chinté parcho na? Oh you fool!
  Can't you recognise me? (*Bengali*).
Ami holam New Zealand théké Maori. Amar haka dékhé
  bujhté parchona? I am a Maori from New Zealand.
  Can't you tell from seeing my *haka*? (*Bengali*).
Nischoi hoté paré Of course it can happen (*Bengali*).
America théké Red Indianra jodhi ashté paré, to New
  Zealand théké Maori lok-o ashté paré If Red Indians
  can come from America, then Maori people can also
  come from New Zealand (*Bengali*).
Hi Greeting. This is accompanied by rubbing noses
  (*Inuit*).
Jani, jani. Eto phorashider babohar I know, I know.
  This is a French custom (*Bengali*).
Bonjour, bonjour. Comment allez-vous? Good day, good
  day. How are you? (*French*).
Conte Count. French title. The female is *Contessa* and
  not *Contestant*, as the gatekeeper believes (*French*).

Marquis Marquis. French title. The female is *Marquise* and not *Marionette* as the gatekeeper believes (*French*).

Sheikh An Arab chief. The female is *sheikha* (*Arabic*).

Eskimodér nak chhoa The nose-rubbing of Eskimos (*Bengali*).

Kojon Eskimo othithi ashé dékhi Let's see how many Eskimo guests turn up (*Bengali*).

Achha, achha! Ebar amar bari Okay, okay! It's my turn now (*Bengali*).

ACT THREE

Coq au vin A French dish, chicken cooked in wine (*French*).

Sushi A Japanese speciality, thin slices of raw fish (*Japanese*).

Mulakhayya A Moroccan green vegetable dish with a slimy texture.

Punkah Fan (*Hindi/Urdu*).

Burfi A dry sweet, like a fudge (*Hindi/Urdu*).

Batao na Do tell (*Hindi/Urdu*).

Open Sesame The password uttered by the forty thieves of *Ali Baba and the Forty Thieves* when they want to open the entrance to their treasure cave.

ACT FOUR

Namasté Greetings (*Hindi*). Also *Namaskar*. This greeting is accompanied by the palms joined together and the head bowed.

Salaam aléikum Muslim greeting, literally meaning 'Peace be upon you.' It is accompanied by lifting the palm to the heart and to the forehead. The customary reply is *walkum assalaam* (*Arabic*).

Walékum assalaam The reply to the usual Muslim greeting, 'And peace be also upon you' (*Arabic*).

Guten morgen Good morning (*German*).

Hola Greetings (*Spanish*).

How American Indian greeting. It is accompanied by a raised palm.

Bonjour Greetings. Literally, 'Good day' (*French*). This is often accompanied by a kiss on both cheeks.

Kombaawa Greetings. This is accompanied by a bow (*Japanese*).

Badmaash Rascal (*Hindi/Urdu*).

Chhor do, mujhé Let me go (*Hindi/Urdu*).

Mujhé under jane do Let me in (*Hindi/Urdu*).

Buddhu Fool (*Hindi/Urdu*).

Bévacoof Idiot (*Hindi/Urdu*).

Ab nikal jao Now be off with you (*Hindi/Urdu*).

Sayonara Goodbye (*Japanese*).

Shalom Goodbye, literally 'Peace' (*Hebrew*).

Khuda Hafiz Goodbye, God be with you (*Urdu*).

Nomoshkar Goodbye (*Bengali*).

Adios Goodbye (*Spanish*).

Achha sa'ab Yes, sir (*Hindi/Urdu*).

Jao! Nikal jao Go! Get out (*Hindi/Urdu*).

Tum jao, uska peechhe karo You go and chase him (*Hindi/Urdu*).

Mujhé thora aaram karné do Let me rest a while (*Hindi/Urdu*).

Maaph kar do, sa'ab Sorry, sir (*Hindi/Urdu*).

Baksheesh A tip (*Arabic/Hindi/Urdu*).

Khoob bhalo Very good (*Bengali*).

Sayonara Goodbye (*Japanese*).

Khuda Hafiz Goodbye, God be with you (*Urdu*).

ACT FIVE

Raj kumar A prince (*Hindi*).

Shahinshah A great ruler, a ruler over rulers (*Farsi/ Hindi/Urdu*).

Badshah King (*Urdu*).

Salaams Respectful greetings (*Arabic/Urdu*).

Swagatam Welcome (*Sanskrit/Hindi*).

Ahalan wa sahalan Welcome (*Arabic*).

Jaci da Greetings, good day (*Welsh*).

Theek hai Okay (*Hindi/Urdu*).

Pukka Genuine (*Hindi/Urdu*).

Eid Muslim festival. The most important Eids are Eid al-Fitr, the festival marking the end of Ramadan or the month of fasting, and Eid al-Adha, the Feast of Sacrifice (*Arabic*).

Mitthai Sweets (*Hindi/Urdu*).

Diwali Hindu festival of light (*Bengali/Hindi/Pujabi*). Also a Sikh festival.

Mishti Sweets (*Bengali*).

Mes amis My friends (*French*).

Méré yaron My friends (*Hindi/Urdu*).

Amar bondhura My friends (*Bengali*).

Amigos mios My friends (*Spanish*).

ACT SIX

Begum Sahiba Lady Madam (*Urdu*).

Jee, Begum Sahiba Yes, Lady Madam (*Urdu*).

Mehndi Henna (*Hindi/Urdu*).

Suno Listen (*Hindi/Urdu*).

Bevacoof Fool (*Hindi/Urdu*).

Begum Sahiba Lady Madam (*Urdu*).

ACT SEVEN

Bohot achha Very good (*Hindi/Urdu*).

Hors d'oeuvres Appetisers, starters (*French*).

Pappadoms Thin, fried savouries (*Hindi/Urdu*).

Kala mirch Black pepper (*Hindi/Urdu*).

Pakoras Fried savouries (*Hindi/Urdu*).

Gobi ka paratha A fried pancake with cauliflower as an ingredient (*Hindi/Urdu*). It is a Punjabi speciality.

Naan A kind of Indian bread (*Hindi/Urdu*).

Senor Mister (*Italian*).

Idlis Savoury rice cakes from South India (*Hindi/Urdu*).

Dhosas Savoury pancakes from South India (*Hindi/Urdu*).

Pilau Rice cooked with ghee (*Hindi/Urdu*).

Basmati A fine quality fragrant rice grown in the Indian sub-continent (*Hindi/Urdu*).

Ghee Clarified butter (*Hindi/Urdu*).

Bhindi Ladies' fingers (*Hindi/Urdu*).

Tinda A round green vegetable (*Hindi/Urdu*).

Vindaloo A hot curry (*Hindi/Urdu*).

Saag-gost Spinach with lamb meat (*Hindi/Urdu*).

Ustad A title meaning an expert or a maestro (*Hindi/Urdu*).

Tikka masalah A spicy curry (*Hindi/Urdu*).

Mishti Sweet (*Bengali*). It is especially apt as the middle name of the Bengali chef since Bengali cooking gives great importance to the preparation of sweets and very many Bengali curries include a pinch of sugar. Bengalis are known for having a sweet tooth.

Rui maach A favourite Bengali fish (*Bengali*).

Ilish maach Another favourite Bengali fish (*Bengali*).

Koi maach Koi fish (*Bengali*).

Pagree Turban (*Bengali/Hindi/Urdu*).

Lassi A buttermilk drink popular in the subcontinent (*Hindi/Urdu*). The same word is *ghol* in Bengali.

Sherbet A refreshing drink (*Hindi/Urdu*).

Uchhkin Waistcoat (*Urdu*).

Masoor dal Red lentils (*Hindi/Urdu*).

Paagal Madman (*Hindi/Urdu*).

Yeh khana mujhe bohot pasand hain This food is very much to my liking (*Hindi/Urdu*).

Baap ré baap Good heavens (*Hindi/Urdu*).

Méri tofa My present (*Hindi/Urdu*).

Mujhé jaldi dé do Quickly, give it to me (*Hindi/Urdu*).

Bohot dafa Many times (*Hindi/Urdu*).

Apsaras Celestial nymphs (*Sanskrit/Hindi*).

Houris Celestial nymphs (*Arabic*).

Merci beaucoup Many thanks (*French*).

Shukriya Thank you (*Hindi/Urdu*).

Shair Poet (*Hindi/Urdu*).

Battameez Brute, scumbag (*Hindi/Urdu*).

DANNY 306 + ME (4EVER)

David Greig

a musical for actors and live animation

For Lucy and Annie

Author's Note

Danny 306 + Me (4ever) came out of a workshop I did
with Nick Barnes. During the workshop Nick introduced
me to his 'Tramp' character. The tramp lived in an old
pushalong basket of the type that people used to use
for their shopping. Suddenly the Tramp came alive and
started talking to Nick and me, howling abuse at us
and chasing us around. Of course, it was all operated
by Nick himself. During the workshop I wrote scenes
for Nick and the Tramp to play, and we discovered that
there is an incredible theatrical potential in using live
animation to tell stories.

Live animation I suppose means puppetry, but that
doesn't really cover it. Puppets usually mean things on
sticks or string whose operators are hidden away
somewhere, or dressed in black so they are unseen.
Nick's genius is to make creations who interact with
their operators. It's this dynamic – between the actor
and the animation – that makes his work so exciting.
It's the stage equivalent of mixing computer animation
with live action.

In *Danny 306* the animations were all different.
Danny himself was a wooden boy, about three feet high,
who was operated by three actors at the same time.
That's why his lines come out in threes – spoken by
his chorus. Because he was operated by three actors,
he could, for example, fly. He was 'animated' with
enormous energy and potential. Mrs McGeever was
a Hoover, with all kinds of terrifying attachments, who
dragged her operator, Beattie, around with demented
fury. And Queenie, the star, was a head and a dress,

always attached to her daughter, weighing her down and keeping her in place.

Danny 306 + Me (4ever) was the product of a very particular collaboration between a writer and an animator. I do hope, however, that the story lives on its own, and perhaps in the future others can find their own ways of bringing these strange and comic creations to life.

Danny 306 + Me (4ever) was first presented by the
Traverse Theatre Company and the Birmingham
Repertory Theatre on 18 May 1999 at the Traverse
Theatre, Edinburgh. The cast was as follows:

Iona Carbarns
Louise Ironside
Ian Skewis
Joel Strachan
Jack McGowan
Callum Cuthbertson
Elaine MacKenzie Ellis

Directed by John Tiffany
Designed by Nick Barnes
Choreography by Marisa Zanotti
Music by Tom Bancroft

Characters

Stella
A young woman, Queenie's daughter

Frank Cream
The hotel manager

Beattie
The chambermaid

Mr Mayakovsky
The chef

Gregory Smirk
The pianist

Lillian
Rico Manhattan's wife

Stanley
Rico Manhattan's son

And, Sandi, Mandi
Working in TV

ANIMATIONS

Queenie
A failed cabaret artiste (*operated and voiced by Stella*)

Danny
A bell-boy (*operated by Sandi, Andi and Mandi*)

Mrs McGeever
An extraordinary cleaning machine (*operated by Beattie*)

Rico Manhattan
A big-time Hollywood producer, six inches tall
(*operated by Lillian*)

Setting

The action takes place initially in the present day
in the derelict Grand Hotel, Cumdoon, Scotland.
Thereafter it takes place in 1929,
when the Grand Hotel is in its heyday.

ONE

Darkness.
  Unseen in the dark, Stella is moving quietly. Humming or singing just audibly.
  Sudden loud voices off, then stumbling around.

Andy Sandi?

Sandi Andy?

Andy Where's Mandi?

Mandi Oh Sandi! Oh Andy!

Andy *and* **Sandi** Mandi?

Mandi I think I've lost her . . .

Sandi *and* **Andy** You've lost her!

Mandi She just wandered off.
  It's so dark.

Andy Well, that's just dandy, Mandi!

Sandi Andy!

Mandi One minute she was there and . . .

Sandi This is a major production. A worldwide network show and we've lost the star!

Andy You've lost the star.

Sandi Let's get some light.
  Does this place have electricity?

Mandi It's so creepy in here.

Andy What if she's dead?

Mandi What's that noise . . .?
Shhh.

The sound of movement.

Sandi Rats.

They all shiver with disgust.

Mandi Nobody's stayed here for years.

Sandi I'll try and find a light switch.

Mandi The rooms are all full of dust.

Andy What if she's fallen through the floor?

Mandi The windows are broken.

Andy The grand old lady of Hollywood is dead.

Mandi It's a dump.

Andy And I killed her.

Sandi She must be somewhere.

Andy My career is over.

Sandi Watch the –

Mandi This is hopeless. (*She trips and yells.*)

Sandi – stairs.

Andy I think I'm going to cry. (*Weeps.*)

Andy I give up. Have you got a tissue or something, Mandi?

Mandi Of course. Here. (*She gives him a tissue.*) Always keep a Handy Andy handy, Andy.

Sandi Stella!

Sandi, Mandi *and* **Andi** Stella!

Mandi Where is the crabby old batface!

> *Stella switches on a light. We see her, old. Quiet.*
> *The foyer of the Grand Hotel.*
> *Old and faded and dusty. Andy, Sandi and Mandi*
> *are a group of twenty-somethings who work for a TV*
> *production company. They're dressed smartly and are*
> *carrying clipboards and personal organisers and all*
> *the paraphernalia of pre-production.*
> *A moment.*
> *They look at her. All blinking in the light.*

Stella Here.

Mandi Stella! Baby. Baby. Thank God.
We thought we'd lost you.

Andy Why don't you sit down, Stella . . . relax?
Where we can see you.
Mandi!

Mandi Andy.

Andy Get Stella a chair. Get her a chair.

> *Stella waves away their advances.*

Mandi Is she okay? Are you okay? You look . . .

Sandi She looks like she's seen a ghost.

Andy Don't tell me this dump's haunted as well?

Mandi It's like we're trapped in an endless episode of
Scooby Doo.

Andy Is this the place, Stella?
Is this where it all began?

Stella This is it.

Mandi Wow.

Andy The place where a career began.

Mandi The place where a legend was born.

Stella has moved over to the piano. Removed some dust. She plays the notes of a tune (the tune she was humming).

Sandi Ancient history.
Look at all this dust.
It'll jam the cameras.

Andy It's unhealthy.
It's doing terrible things to Mandi's complexion.

Stella is exploring.
  She starts to walk up the staircase towards the mirror . . .

Sandi Uh-oh. The lady's gone tweet-tweet.

Andy Loopy-loo.

Mandi I refuse to work in these conditions.

Sandi Okay. People, this is our location. This is the place. Lets make some TV!

Mandi Let's do lunch. I'm upset. I have to do lunch now.

Andy The Grand Hotel.
Cumdoon. Scotland.

Sandi Let's shoot some shots.
Let's make this old wreck presentable.

Andy Okay. Mandi – make up time . . .

Sandi I mean the hotel. Tidy up the hotel.

Mandi Come on, Stella.
We'll do the interview here.

She is looking at Danny, who has appeared in the mirror.

Stella I knew you'd be here.
It's me.
I came back.
I promised I would, didn't I?

Sandi Okay. People. Okay!
I want this place to look just like it would have when Stella first came here in . . .

Stella Nineteen twenty-nine.

Sandi Nineteen twenty-whatever.
So . . .
So . . . it would have looked . . .

Mandi Well, it would have looked . . .

Andy It would have looked . . .

Stella Grand.
It would have looked grand.

She points to a sepia photograph hanging on the wall. It's a photograph of Mr Frank Cream looking proprietorial in front of the stairs.
    Music begins from a piano under a dust sheet.

IN AN OLD PHOTOGRAPH

In an old photograph you can see it
The ghost of a different time
The mahogany's dusted
And the lift isn't busted
And the fwoi-yer is ever so posh, don't you know,
Where an elegant chap plays the grand piano.

Dust sheet removed. Gregory revealed. He coughs.

Gregory Oh. Young people. How . . . unpleasant.

I was rather expecting an altogether better class of audience . . .

Ah well.

One is an artiste.

One struggles on.

In an old photograph you can see it
How they lived in a different time
When a train meant a steam one
And a tea meant a cream one
And a treat meant a trip out to sunny Cumdoon
For candyfloss, bright lights and views of Dunoon.

In an old photograph you can see it
The way that the world once was
No Adidas, no Nike
No TV – oh crikey!
No PCs or CDs or Play-Station games
So kids sat at home and read books when it rained.

Danny, I know I look old now
Danny, I'm faded and grey
But Danny, this old skin might just be a dustsheet
Danny, it might fall away.

And Danny, would you still remember?
Danny, who would you see?
Would you see an antique all covered in dust
Or Danny, would you see me?

*Frank Cream enters with a camera on a stand and a
black hood.*
    Beattie is with him.

Frank This, Beattie, has come direct from Paris.

It is the very latest in photographic technology.

Beattie What do you want me to do with it, Mr Cream?

Frank Stand it over there, Beattie.
  Now, how do I look?

Beattie Very smart, Mr Cream. Very . . . modern.

  Take a new photograph and we'll capture
  The glamour, the grace and the style
  Cummerbunds must be tight ones
  And cuffs just the right ones.

Beattie You look smashing, Mr C.

  And hair must be oiled and shoes must be buffed
  Now straighten your bow tie and smile, and look
    chuffed.

  Take a picture so we can remember
  When we were all in our prime
  In our youth, in our cups
  Gay old dogs, mad young pups
  The world is your oyster, I'm your wee lemon slice
  Come on quick take a pic of the world while it's nice.

Frank Pimm's, Beattie?

Beattie Yes please, Mr Cream . . .

Frank On the rocks?

Beattie No, just here by the piano's fine, thanks.

Frank Snifter, Gregory?

Gregory Please.

Beattie I'll need to watch myself, Mr Cream. One of
these and I come over all flirtatious.

Gregory Give mine to Beattie.

Frank Ordinarily, Beattie, you don't see me letting my
hair down in front of the staff.
  But this is a special occasion.

Gregory Go mad, Mr Cream, go mad.

Frank To the new summer season at the Grand!

Beattie *and* **Gregory** Cheers.

> Take a picture so we can remember
> The year nineteen twenty-nine
> Oh the fabulous frocks
> And the drinks on the rocks
> And your life happens once and it don't happen twice
> So come on quick take a pic of the world while it's
> nice.
>
> And your life happens once and it don't happen twice
> Come on quick take a pic of the world while it's nice.

A camera flash.
   Blackout.

TWO

The reception bell tings and the picture comes to life.
   Queenie enters with Stella.

Queenie Stella dear, I'm dead on my feet. I really am.
They could have given us a porter at the station, couldn't
they? I said to them, 'I am a lady. I am in distress. I require
a porter to carry my bags.' But it was all rudeness.
Rudeness. Sour faces. As if everyone in the world was
sucking lemons, truly. It's just not elegant, is it? And I
did tell you to cry. If a little girl cries everyone suddenly
becomes nice again. That's something I've noticed. You
should have cried when I told you to. Then we'd have got
a porter. They'd have said, 'Look at the poor weeping
child,' and we'd have had a hundred porters, Stella.
They'd have carried us on their trolleys to the door of
the hotel. They'd have carried us head-high like we were
aristocracy, Stella. And I would not have sore feet now.

So think about that.
Is that a spot?

Stella Mum. Please.

Queenie Your hair, it's dull, Stella.
Your complexion, it's pasty.
You hide yourself behind your hair like an ugly mouse.
And now you have a spot.
Can't you try to be glamorous, darling. Why do you have to be so . . . so . . . wooden!

Stella I'm sorry . . . I . . . I'm only . . .

Queenie The Grand Hotel, Cumdoon.
Hmm.
If this is Grand, I'm the Queen of Sheba.
Another summer season singing in a shabby seaside hotel.
I don't know if I can bear it.
I deserve better.
I do it for you, my darling. I hope you're grateful.
Now.
Let's get some service.

She rings the bell. Frank Cream appears at the top of the stairs and hurries down to them.

Frank Ladies. Ladies . . . welcome.
How may I help you?

Queenie I want to speak to the manager.

Frank That's me. Frank Cream. Very pleased to meet you. (*He kisses her hand.*)

Queenie Queenie Trotter.

Frank Oh. Oh. Good Lord. Forgive me.
Queenie Trotter.

The Queenie Trotter.
Stands before me. In all her – glory.
I bow. I kneel. I . . . kiss your feet . . . where are your feet?

Queenie Keep looking, they're in there somewhere.

Frank But of course, she walks on air . . .
I can't . . . can I just . . . because I don't believe it.
Queenie Trotter.
I saw you when you sang at the Ritz in London . . .
I'm a fan.
It's such a privilege to have you singing at our establishment.

Queenie It's a pleasure to be in such a . . . cosy place.

Frank The premier establishment on the Ayrshire Riviera.

Queenie Quite.
If you don't mind me saying so, Mr Cream . . .
You're a little – young – to be the manager.

Frank I inherited this place, Miss Trotter.
My family have run hotels in Scotland since my great-great-grandmother Morag McCrum played host to the entire Jacobite army in her tiny bothy in Glenshee with only a drawer full of porridge in the larder. And you know, they all left completely satisfied.

Queenie I can imagine.
Quite a heroic lady.

Frank Hospitality is in my blood.
There's nothing I'd rather do than provide my guests with the supreme, the luxury, the top-notch, five-star, *pièce de la résistance*, *crême de la crême*, or should I say, cream de la cream of service.

Queenie (*snootily examining the decor*) Well, at least you try.

Frank Please, please, you must be tired after your journey.

Can I arrange for you and – good lord – who is this young lady? I hardly noticed her hiding behind her mother's skirts there like a timid wee . . . mouse.

Queenie (*thrusting her forward*) Introduce yourself, darling.

Stella (*mumbling*) I'm Stella.

Queenie Speak up!

Frank Aww . . . she's shy.

Queenie Project! Stella.

Stella I'm Stella.

Frank She's overawed by her surroundings.

Queenie I sincerely hope not.

Frank Now, ladies, I've been remiss – I have neglected to offer you something to eat . . .

Queenie Gin and tonic.

Stella Mum . . . it's only lunchtime.

Queenie And a sandwich.

Frank And the young lady?

Stella Who, me? Oh. Ehm. Anything. Thank you . . .

Frank I'll just see if the chef can rustle up something. Mr Mayakovsky!

The kitchen comes alive.
It is a frenzy of activity, of chopping and mincing and slicing.

Mr Mayakovsky Donald – carrots.

Donald Yes, sir. Carrots, sir . . .

Frank I wonder if you could make these ladies a little sandwich.

Mr Mayakovsky I'm making soup. Lovely soup to my own recipe.

Frank Mr Mayakovsky, we have guests.

Mr Mayakovsky Kippers, eels, squid, semolina . . .

Donald Slow down, sir, you're chopping too fast.
He's chopping too fast.

Mr Mayakovsky Lamb, beef, pork . . .

Frank The ladies would just like a little snack.

Donald Mr Cream, he's chopping everything.

Mr Mayakovsky Avocado, courgette . . .

Donald He's chopping the kitchen to pieces.

Mr Mayakovsky Brussels sprout, a table, Donald's finger.

Frank Perhaps Donald could . . .

Donald No. No. Not my finger!

Mr Mayakovsky Chop chop chop.
Lovely soup, delicious ingredients.

Donald Aaarrrggghhh.

Frank slams the kitchen hatch shut.

Frank Chef's busy, I'm afraid.
He's worked at the top hotels of Europe you know.
We're lucky to have him.
But he can be . . . temperamental.

Perhaps if I arrange for a sandwich to be brought to your room?

Queenie Just bring me a gin and tonic, darling, and be quick about it.

Frank Of course, of course.
You must be tired.

Queenie Tired? I can hardly stand. Stella here's holding me up!

Frank Please let me take you through to the bar.
I'll call the boy to carry your luggage.
Danny! Danny!

Queenie You stay there, darling, I won't be long.
Mr Cream and I are just going to . . . talk business.

Frank leaves with Queenie.

Frank It really is such an honour to have you.
You'll bring the guests flocking.
I know you will.
Your season here will be a glorious success.

Queenie Not too much tonic in the gin, young man, it gives me a headache.

Danny arrives at the top of the stairs.
Stella is standing with a suitcase.

Danny Mr Cream. Called me. Get your suitcase. Is it?

Stella . . .

Danny slides down the banister and lands at Stella's feet.

Danny I'm Danny. The bellboy, the kitchen boy, the odd-job man . . . Who're you? You on holiday?

Stella My mother's the singer.

I'm here for the summer.
You're supposed to take our suitcase to our room.

Danny Right-oh. No problem. Consider it done. (*He offers bag of sweets.*) Soor ploom? Bonbon? Gobstopper?

Stella What?

Danny D'you want some bubble gum. 'S from America. Man gave it me.
Only been chewed five times. I've had it for two weeks.

Stella I'm not allowed chewing gum.
My mum says it makes my face go ugly.

Danny Suit yourself. What's in here, then . . .
Any scran? Any games? Any money?

He's about to look in the suitcase. She stops him.

Stella What are you doing! Stop that!

Danny Hold your horses. Keep your hair on. Don't get your knickers in a twist.
I'm only having fun.

Stella Well . . . well . . . don't. Please.

He takes the suitcase.

Danny You coming, then? Or. You staying there?

Stella I have to stay here and wait for my mother.

Danny Suit yourself. I'll see you later. Show you around.

Stella I don't think I should . . .

Danny How not?

Stella Mother says I'm not to mix with . . .

Danny Ooooohhhh . . .

Stella I didn't mean . . .

Danny You'll see me. Can't not. Not in this place.
This is my patch.
See you later.

*Danny exits, in an over-elaborate way. Stella can't
help but be impressed.*
*Beattie and Mrs McGeever with the trolley: they
maniacally whizz about cleaning.*

Mrs McGeever Spotless, Beattie, I want this place.
Spotless.

Beattie Mrs McGeever, slow down.

Mrs McGeever Dusted. Polished. Shining. Gleaming.

Beattie I'm exhausted . . .

Mrs McGeever Buff, Beattie! Buff like your life depends
on it.
If it moves. Buff it.
If it's stuck down. Buff it anyway!

Beattie I can't go on.

Mrs McGeever Oh, you're a disappointment to me,
lassie.
I thought you had the makings in you – I thought you
had steel, Beattie.

Beattie I'm trying, Mrs McG, but . . .

Mrs McGeever But nothing.
I can see I'm going to have to take you in hand.

Beattie Oh God.
Oh . . . Mrs McGeever, here comes a guest.

Mrs McGeever A what?

Beattie A guest . . .

Guest Excuse me, I wonder if I could book a room . . .

Mrs McGeever GET OFF MY CLEAN FLOOR – NOW.
YA VANDAL. YA HOOLIGAN.

Beattie Mrs McGeever! What are you doing?

Mrs McGeever I'LL HAVE NO GUESTS ON MY
FLOOR.
GET OUT. GET OUT . . .
GET OUT.

Guest Excuse me! I'll take my business elsewhere . . .

Mrs McGeever Look at the state of you.
Smarten yourself up.
Smarten up those filthy shoes.
And those filthy clothes.
My God, son, you look like you've been dragged
through the heather backwards.
The state of your face.
Beattie – buff him!

Beattie Oh no . . .

Mrs McGeever Buff this man's head!

Beattie I'm awfy sorry. I'm going to have to buff your
head.

They buff the Guest's head.

Mrs McGeever That's better.
Now . . .
What do you want?

Guest I have never been so humiliated in all my life!

Mrs McGeever You were filthy. You had a filthy head.
And now it's shiny again.

Guest I'm leaving. I'll stay somewhere else. In a tent.

Anywhere but this – circus. (*Guest leaves. Incredulous.*)
You . . . you buffed my head!

Mrs McGeever See, Beattie, that's an example. You'll
find this, working with guests. They've no manners.

> *Somewhere on Mrs McGeever's person an alarm rings.*

Cup of tea. Cup of tea. Cup of tea.
  Must have cup of tea.

Beattie But Mrs McGeever, we're supposed to be
working.

Mrs McGeever You stay where you are, lassie.
  Don't move a muscle.

Beattie Why not.

Mrs McGeever Because, Beattie, we are on a tea break.

> *They set about making a cup of tea for themselves
> and drinking it.*
>   *Mr Gregory Smirk arrives.*

Gregory Good morning all.

Beattie Good morning, Gregory.

Gregory Beattie, I must say you look radiant today.

> *Gregory goes over to Mr Mayakovsky.*

Mrs McGeever You're blushing.

Beattie No I'm not.

Mrs McGeever You've got a great big beamer.

Beattie It's just a bit warm in here.

Mrs McGeever (*finger to her face*) Tsssssss.
  You fancy him.

Gregory Good morning, Mr Mayakovsky, how are you today?

The sound of sobbing.

Mr Mayakovsky?

Mr Mayakovsky I'm depressed.

Gregory I'm sorry to hear that.

Mr Mayakovsky I chopped up Donald's finger.
I put it in the soup.

Gregory Oh dear.
Is Donald hurt?
I can see that would make you depressed.

Mr Mayakovsky It's not that.
I'm depressed because his flavour ruins the soup.
He was a plooky little Scottish boy.
Not a healthy specimen.
I can't serve this.
Taste it.

Gregory Tastes alright to me.

Mr Mayakovsky I have standards.
Only the finest ingredients.
Donald's finger was not fine.
I don't even know where it's been.
It tastes a little bit . . . off. I'll have to make new soup.
DONALD! DONALD!
I want to make more soup.

Donald Oh God, Mr Mayakovsky . . . please . . . no chopping . . . no chopping . . .

Gregory shuts the kitchen hatch.

Gregory A cup of tea would be lovely if you're making, Mrs McGeever.

They all sit still.
  Frank Cream comes out briefly.
  They suddenly rush to seem busy.

Frank Everybody working hard out here. Good. Good.

All Yes, Mr Cream, very busy.

Mrs McGeever GIT AFF MA CLEAN FLOOR, YA DIRTY BEGGAR!

Frank DON'T BUFF ME! (*He cowers momentarily.*)
  Now. I am entertaining a very important new member of staff so . . .

Queenie More gin! I'll not sing unless I get more gin.

Frank Just so you're all busy.

Gregory Oh, all busy, sir.

Beattie Working hard.

Frank Good. (*to Stella*) Enjoying your stay, Stella?
  Your mother really is a delight.
  I'm sure you'll feel very at home here.
  You know we like to joke, don't we, staff . . .?

Staff No.

Frank We like to say – you don't have to be mad to work here . . .
  But it helps.

  A scream from the kitchen.

Donald He's killed the dog! He's killed the dog!

Mr Mayakovsky Don't worry, Donald, it adds body to the soup.

Frank It really does. It really does help.

Stella (*sings*)

WHERE THE HELL IS THIS?

Do you ever ever ever look at persons
As the situa-ua-ua-uation worsens
Now I'm truly very sorry if I'm cursin
But where oh where oh where the hell is this?

The chambermaid's a lunatic dictator
They plug her in and switch her on and then inflate her
The crazy bellboy's coming back to see me later
Oh tell me where oh where oh where the hell is this?

I've been in Berwick, Largs and Ayr
I've stayed in awful places where
The rooms were damp and stank of salesmen's
    sweaty socks
Stayed with a very creepy fellow
At some digs in Portobello
Who wore a kilt and gave me several nasty shocks.

The chef's a very dangerous psychotic
The way the place is run is just chaotic
I'm sorry if you think I am neurotic
But where oh where oh where the hell is this?

Been in Clacton and in Brighton
Stayed a season or a night in
Every place from here to flipping John o' Groats
Don't want another summer season
Where the weather's always freezin
And we haven't got a peg to hang our coats.

I'm confused and I just want to get my bearings
Been in so many places I'm past caring
The fabric of my sanity is tearing
Where oh where oh where oh where . . .
Because I must be dreaming.

There must be some mistake.
Tell me it's an elaborate practical joke
Just tell me where oh where oh where the hell is this?

Queenie (*from off*) Stella! Stella! Darling, I'm stuck on a barstool and I can't get off.

Stella She . . . has a . . . bad back.

*Stella goes off and brings her now tipsy mother on.
Leads her upstairs to bed.*
   Beattie and Mrs McGeever watch the procedure.

Beattie Poor woman. Looks like an awfy bad back she's got.

Mrs McGeever Gets it from sitting on those barstools.

Stella Careful, Mum.

Queenie You're a lovely lassie. Isn't she a lovely wee lassie? She's that . . . good to me. Goodnight, Mr Cream. He's a lovely young man. He's that lovely . . . A piano. A piano . . . I want to sing.

Stella Time for a sleep, Mum.

Queenie I was born to sing. 'S all I can do. Where's the audience? I want to give them my talent . . . this place is a dump. A pit. A dive. I've sang at the Ritz. Have I told you . . .

Stella You've told me.

Queenie I'm tired. I feel sick. What are we doing in a place like this, darling? We deserve better.

Stella It's alright, Mum, it's better than nothing.

Queenie It's lovely. What a lovely man. I like these little places. I'm a travelling artiste. A nightingale for hire. I love this place. I want to sing! She's a lovely lassie.

I'm so proud of my lassie. Where's the audience? Where's the people? I know it's going to be all right, darling. I know we're going to like it here. Already I feel right . . . at home.

Lights down.

THREE

The next morning.
Beattie and Mrs McGeever enter.

Mrs McGeever Beattie! Gird your loins. We've got work to do.
Cutlery to polish. Tables to be set. Beds to make. Sheets to crisp.

Beattie I resign. I'm too tired. I can't do it.

Mrs McGeever First – vacuum cleaning. Switch on.

The vacuum cleaner switches on. Beattie can barely control it.

Beattie It's very powerful, Mrs McGeever . . .

Mrs McGeever Turn it up.

Beattie I can hardly control it . . .

Mrs McGeever YOU NEED STEEL IN YOUR SOUL, BEATTIE.
TURN IT UP. UP. UP.

Beattie is being tossed around by the Hoover hose, which is bent on destroying everything that comes near it . . .
Frank Cream comes out of his office, impelled by the Hoover's immense suction.

Frank Oh God, Mrs McGeever, switch it off, switch it off, please.

Beattie He's being sucked in.
Hold on, sir. Hold on!

Frank The alarm, Beattie. The alarm.

Beattie What?

Mrs McGeever I WILL BUFF I WILL BUFF I WILL BUFF.

Frank Tea break!

Beattie realises. Sets off the tea break alarm. Mrs McGeever calms down again. The Hoover stops.

Mrs McGeever Cup of tea. Cup of tea. Cup of tea.

Frank Good Lord, it's very . . . efficient, Mrs McGeever.
That vacuum. I was very nearly entombed within its fearsome jaw, myself, there.

Mrs McGeever Mr Cream. Nothing escapes it. Nothing. Nothing at all.

Frank Good. Well. Good.
Oh God.

Frank exits.
Mrs McGeever produces the tea and biscuits and relaxes.

Mrs McGeever Did you do anything nice last night, Beattie?

Beattie Mr Smirk took me to the pictures.

Mrs McGeever You fancy him.

Beattie No.

Mrs McGeever You fancy him something rotten.

Beattie I just think he's a very interesting person.

Mrs McGeever You fancy him something so rotten it's been down the back of the couch for six months.

Beattie He was very romantic. We walked hand in hand along the promenade.

Mrs McGeever Did he try it on?

Beattie He said poetry to me.

Mrs McGeever Did he kiss you?

Beattie He was the perfect gentleman.

Mrs McGeever Not even a peck?

Beattie No.

Mrs McGeever Chuck him. He's useless. Ditch him.

Frank Cream enters with Lilian and Stanley.
Mrs McGeever suddenly inflates.

Frank NO. NO. SWITCH HER OFF FOR GOD'S SAKE!

Beattie Yes, sir. Sorry, sir.

Frank We've got very important guests.
I don't want them sucked into the belly of that evil beast.

They move towards the exit, surreptitiously listening to the dialogue.

Lilian This has to be top secret, Mr Cream.

Frank Oh it will be. I assure you.

Stanley Do you have a golf course?
Dad likes to play golf.

Frank Cumdoon is blessed with an excellent five-star golf course.
  With views of the sea.

Lilian Is it windy? Is it rainy?

Stanley Dad doesn't like wind.

Lilian He doesn't like rain.

Frank Well, you'll find here the weather occasionally can be inclement . . .

Lilian Well unclement it.
  I don't want my Rico catching pneumonia.

Frank It's not really possible to . . .

Lilian Mr Cream, I should make you aware that Mr Rico Manhattan is a big Hollywood producer . . .

Stanley The biggest.

Lilian He invented the talkie.

Stanley Can you believe that – movies where people talk.

Lilian And the walkie.

Stanley Movies where people walk.

Lilian And the walkie-talkie.

Stanley Where they do both at the same time.

Lilian My husband is a giant.

Stanley He's big.

Lilian So if I tell you Rico Manhattan wants to play golf in the sunshine. You get me sunshine.

Frank We'll certainly try . . .
  Please, let me show you the rest of the facilities . . .

Lilian, Stanley and Frank exit.

Beattie A Hollywood producer's coming to stay!
A big producer.
The big producer.
Isn't that exciting?
He might spot us.

Mrs McGeever He'll not spot you, Beattie.

Beattie Why not?

Mrs McGeever You're not shiny enough.
Movie stars have to be shiny people.
With shiny faces.

Beattie No . . . Mrs McGeever, no.

Mrs McGeever And shiny heads . . .

Beattie Please . . .

Mrs McGeever I WILL BUFF YOU. I WILL BUFF
YOU . . .

Beattie exits pursued by a crazed Mrs McGeever.
Pause.
From upstairs, unseen:

Queenie OH GOD.
OH GOD.
Oh God, darling. My head feels like the Battle of the
Somme. I can't get up. Leave me alone. Switch the lights
off. Bring me an aspirin. Bring me a new head!

*Stella appears at the top of the stairs. She is dressed in
quite a prissy way. She walks down and sits in the
foyer.*
Danny enters with a bag of laundry.

Danny Hiya. Morning. Howdy, pardner.

Stella Oh, it's you.

Danny Your mum giving you gip? Banging on? Yelling?
Wish she'd shut up.
She'll wake up the guests.
Keep the noise down, missus.
Why you dressed like that?
Posh. You going to a wedding? To a funeral?
Off to meet the Queen?

Stella This is how my mum wants me to dress.

Danny No use for the beach. No use for swimming. No
use for mucking about.

Stella I don't do any of those things.
That's for kids.

Danny What's your name anyway?

Stella . . .

Danny It's secret? You can tell me, babe.
Da broad came inta my office . . .
This is my Jimmy Cagney.
She didn't say what her name was. She was fulla
secrets.
I told her – Baby, I'm a detective not a mind-reader . . .
I can get into the pictures. Without paying. There's
a door you can sneak through.
I'll show you.
What's your name?

Stella Stella.

Danny Stella. Stellie. Stel. Stelster.
If you're here for the summer, you'd better stick with
me.
I'm the expert in this place.
Everyone else is off their heads.

Stella I know. I've seen.

Danny First thing's first.
I'll dump the laundry with Mrs McGeever.
Then it's my afternoon off.
C'mon, follow me.

Stella No. I can't.

Danny Why not?

Stella I'm not allowed.

Danny Forget that. Have a laugh. C'mon.
I'll show you around – you're new – let you see the sights.
Show you where the best birds' nests are. Show you the place where the rocks make a noise. Show you where Mr McIvor lives in a hut – with skulls.

Stella It's a bit immature, isn't it?

Danny What's that mean? Immature? What's that?

Stella My mum wouldn't approve.

Danny Don't have no – immature – at the Grand.

Stella She doesn't like me playing.

Danny Don't like it. So. Do it anyway.

THE WORLD BELONGS TO ME

Danny
Forget your mum for just a little while

Stella
I can't

Danny
Just disobey, do what you fancy, smile

Stella

    I really can't

Danny

    I'll show you how to have a laugh in style

Stella

    No really, I can't

Danny

    Why be an adult? Just be juvenile . . .

Danny

    I don't have nobody tellin me what to do
    I don't have nobody telling me stupid rules
    Don't go to school
    Just play it cool
    I'm absolutely free
    Don't have two pennies to rub together
    But the world belongs to me.

    Come on, let's kick stones along the streets.

Stella

    I wish I could . . .

Danny

    We'll fish for crabs and sell them to buy sweets

Stella

    If only . . .

Danny

    We'll jump off sand dunes and do daredevil feats

Stella

    Well . . .

Danny

    What's the use of life without no treats?
    I don't have nobody tellin me what to do

I don't have nobody telling me stupid rules
Don't go to school
Just play it cool
I'm absolutely free
Don't have two pennies to rub together
But the world belongs to me.

Look at the world
It's full of brilliant places
There's rafts to build
And beaches to run races
There's dens to make
And tricks to play
And trams to jump
And every day
A new place to go fishin.

Stella

I wish I could but
I haven't got permission.

Danny

I don't have nobody tellin me what to do
I don't have nobody telling me stupid rules
Don't go to school
Just play it cool
I'm absolutely free
Don't have two pennies to rub together
But the world belongs to me.

It's easy, just believe it in your head.

Stella

Maybe.

Danny

Do what you want tomorrow you might be dead

Stella
    I suppose.

Danny
    Who wants to listen to what their mother said.

Stella
    Well . . .

Danny
    Why grow up when you can be a kid instead?

Both
    I don't have nobody telling me what to do
    I don't have nobody telling me stupid rules
    Don't go to school
    Just play it cool
    I'm absolutely free
    Don't have two pennies to rub together but the
    world belongs to me.

Queenie
    DARLING, WHERE'S MY ASPIRIN?
    DARLING, I'M DYING. I'M NOT LONG FOR
    THIS WORLD.

Stella I really shouldn't.

Danny But you will.

    Danny exits, Stella follows.
        Stanley, Lilian and Frank enter.

Stanley Dad only eats burgers – can you do burgers . . . ?

Frank I'll ask the chef.
    One moment.
    Erm . . . Mr . . . Mr Mayakovsky . . .

    *Frank opens the kitchen hatch. Steam pours out. Mr
    Mayakovsky is discovered shouting.*

Stanley I think this place'll be okay.

Mr Mayakovsky Where is Donald?

Donald I resign. I'm not working for you any more.

Lilian I hope Rico takes a rest.

Mr Mayakovsky What do you mean? I am a chef of genius. You are my apprentice.

Donald I've no fingers left. You make soup again there'll be nothing left of me at all.

Stanley It's quiet here. Nobody knows Dad.

Lilian We've got to stop him working.
   He mustn't exert himself.

Stanley Whatever happens we'll make sure he has a relaxing holiday.

Mr Mayakovsky You lazy son of a Siberian yak-herd.

Donald I resign. I want my wages.

Frank Mr Mayakovsky!

Mr Mayakovsky Boss! How can I help?

Frank We have a very important guest.
   He only eats burgers. American-style. Can you do that?

Mr Mayakovsky No problem, Mr Cream!
   I do burgers any style you like.

Frank Excellent.

Mr Mayakovsky Even Scottish style.

Frank Terrific – he does burgers Scottish-style . . .

Mr Mayakovsky Try one.
   Donald!

Donald Ah ah noo nooo.
  I resign. I resign.

  Mincing machine.

Mr Mayakovsky Too late – you're fired.
  Or should I say
  Flame grilled?

  Noise of frying.
    A burger with a pair of spectacles on it comes out.

One, unique, Chef Mayakovsky designed . . .
  Scottish-style burger.
  I call it after it's chief ingredient.
  MacDonald's.

  Frank hurriedly shuts the hatch.
    Queenie has appeared at the top of the stairs. She observes what's going on below.

Frank Uhm. Our chef says he can certainly do burgers for you.
  That will be no problem at all.

Lilian Okay. Good. I think we'll stay.
  We'll book a suite.
  Two suites.
  Remember, Mr Cream.
  This is top secret.
  I don't want Rico Manhattan being bothered when he's on holiday.
  Come on, Stanley.
  Let's go.

Stanley This burger is terrific, Mom.
  I think this could be the best I've ever tasted.

Lilian Top secret, Mr Cream. Not a word to anyone.

  They exit.

Queenie Hollywood . . . hold on to your hats. Queenie Trotter, the Newton Mearns Nightingale . . . is about to be discovered!

She exits.
Lights down.

FOUR

Later.
Queenie, Frank, Gregory Smirk and Beattie.
Queenie is checking that everything is prepared.

Frank Queenie . . . he really doesn't want to be bothered.

Queenie Are you suggesting my singing will 'bother' him?

Beattie Oh, I love Rico Manhattan films.
I love the dancing.
I wish I could be in one.

Queenie Well, you can't.

Gregory What tempo would you like me to play, Ms Trotter?

Queenie Slow . . . I think, Gregory . . . slow . . .
Now . . .
We'll place Mr Manhattan over there.
Does my dress look right?
My hair?

Frank You look divine, Queenie.

Queenie So kind. And yet . . . so accurate . . . I do look divine.

Beattie I can dance.
   Do you think he'll discover me?

Queenie Not unless he looks under a stone. Now.
   Everyone ready for a practice.
   Note, Gregory.
   Ahhhhh, ahhhh, ahhhh.

Beattie and Mrs McGeever grimace.

Gregory.

Gregory What?

Queenie Give me a note.

Gregory Terribly sorry, I thought you were choking.

Queenie I was singing C.

Gregory Good God, were you?.
   Count me in.

Gregory One, two, three, four . . .

THE LADY CAN'T SING

Queenie
   Ever since I was a little girl
   I had a little dream
   To see my name up there in lights
   And on the silver screen
   The fans that would surround me
   And demand my autograph
   But when I tell folk of my dream
   They always seem to laugh.

All
   She's got class, she's got style and
   Her tail's got one hot sting

Gregory

    Which makes it most unfortunate
    That the lady just can't sing.

Queenie

    I long to be queen of them all
    And play Carnegie Hall
    To be voted best actress
    At the Oscar ball
    I'll steal Fred from Ginger
    And dance without a care
    And the stars will stop
    And their jaws will drop
    When they hear my vocal flair

All

    She's got class, she's got style and
    She's got that zhuzhy thing

Gregory

    It really is a tragedy
    But the lady just can't sing

Queenie

    La, la, la, la, la, la, la

All

    She can't sing a note

Queenie

    La, la, la, la, la, la, la

All

    She's got a frog in her throat

Queenie

    La, la, la, la, la, la, la

All

    She's got a voice like a cat howling
    She can dance, she can act
    She can fly – that's a fact
    She's got class, she's got style
    And the girl can really swing

Gregory

    I wish it were otherwise
    But the lady just can't sing

Queenie

    Now I'm not a little girl any more
    But I've still got my little dream
    And I know I'll see my name in lights
    And on the silver screen
    And fans they will surround me
    And demand my autograph
    And then, you'll see, it will be me
    That has the last damn laugh.

    I've got class, I've got style
    I'm one very zhuzhy miss
    My name is Queenie Trotter
    Best wishes, kiss, kiss, kiss.

FIVE

Later that evening, Danny and Stella tumble back in from the beach. Her clothes are messy.

Stella Did you see Old Mr McIvor's face!

Danny This is my. Favourite. Skull.
    I think. It's. Quite recent.

Stella (*shivers*) I know they're only animal bones.
    But it was still creepy.

Danny He's okay. I've known him for ever. He just collects.

And wasn't it brilliant? When we were on the ferry. And you told the ticket collector . . .

Stella (*recreates being upset*) Sorry, mister, our tickets blew out of our hands and fell into the sea . . .

Danny You were great. He even gave us the best seats on deck.

You're an actress.

Stella Learned it all from my mum.

You got any sweets left?

Danny Loads. Gobstopper. Biggest I've got.

Stella puts the gobstopper in her mouth.

Stella Umph gumph glub flub . . . (*Thanks, Danny – today was special.*)

Danny What?

Stella Umph gumph glub flub. (*Today was special. Takes gobstopper out.*) Thanks, Danny, for –

Danny Don't matter. I know. We're pals.

Stella But I –

Danny Umph gumph. Glub flub. 'S all you need to say.

I've got to work tomorrow.

But we can go out again at the weekend.

Stella Aren't you too young to work?

Danny Don't be daft. I do everything round here. I'm head waiter. I'm laundry boy. I climb up on the roof and take dead pigeons out of the gutters. I do the lot. I run this place. You ever need anything, Stellster. Anything at all. You need something done or something seen to – ask me. I'm the boss.

Stella Lucky I met you then. Always good to be in with the boss.

Danny Tell you the truth, Stellster, I'm glad you're here. 'Cos it's boring with just me about. The others are okay, but – they're not kids. We'll have fun this summer. You're alright. First I thought you were stuck up. But now I think. You'll do.

Stella I've had the best time, Danny.
I've never done that anything like that before.

Danny What – muck about? Laugh? Have fun?

Stella Didn't know I could.

Danny You do now.

Stella sings.

Stella
I don't have nobody telling me what to do.

Danny Yeah. That's it.

Stella
I don't have nobody laying down stupid rules.

Danny You got the hang of it.

Stella
Don't go to school. Just play it cool. I'm absolutely free.

Danny Free and easy.

Stella
Don't have two pennies to rub together but the world belongs to me.

Danny Wow, Stellster. You're good.

Stella I wish I was.

Danny You are.

Stella I'm rubbish really.

Danny Don't say that. Don't you dare say that.

Stella What?

Danny Rubbish. Call yourself rubbish.

Stella Sorry, I just . . .

Danny Never say it.
You don't know what it means to be rubbish.
You know nothing.

Stella I didn't mean to upset you.

Danny 'S alright. Forget it. Never mind.
Leave it. 'S nothing. 'S finished.

Awkwardness.

Stella Where are your parents, Danny?

Danny Don't have none.

Stella You must have some, somewhere.

Danny I was just found.
In a room.
Found me in a waste-paper basket in room 306.
Wrapped in a hotel towel. So I don't have no mum and
I don't have no dad and I don't have no brothers and
I don't have no sisters and that's just the way I like it.
Danny 306.
Me and my pals.
Against the world.

Stella Poor Danny.

Danny Not poor Danny. Lucky Danny.

Stella No mum though . . .

Danny Look at yours. She shouts. That's worse.

Stella She doesn't mean it.
  She does her best.
  It can't be easy with . . . me.

Danny What's wrong with you?

Stella Me? Isn't it obvious? Everything.
  I'd better go and find her.
  She'll be angry with me. Running off like that.
  Suppose I'll just have to face the music.

Danny Do you want back-up? I'll sort you . . .

Stella No. I know how to handle her. I'm the only
person who does.

Danny See you later, Stella.

Stella Danny.
  Thanks for . . .

Danny Umph gumph. Flub glub.
  Don't need to say.

Stella goes to kiss him. He flinches.

Oi! What you doing, slobbering? You my granny or
something?
  Leave off.

Stella Sorry.

Danny Typical girl.
  I'm off. Grab some shut-eye. I'm a working man.
Need my kip.
  Night, Stellster.

Stella Night, Danny 306.
  Sleep well.

Danny leaves.
   A voice from off.
   It's Queenie.

Queenie Not too much tonic in the gin, young man!

Stella Oh, Mum.

   She goes over to the bar. Queenie is there with
   Gregory Smirk.

Queenie Stella. Darling. Where've you been? Running off. I'm going to be discovered tomorrow. It's my big day. Where were you?

Stella I was . . . with a friend.

Queenie A friend, darling? You don't have friends. Who'd like an ugly mouse like you? Anyway, my darling, I'm taking you away from all this. Hollywood. It's all planned. You'll have a better class of friend. A better class altogether.
   Now you scoot off to bed.
   Mr Smirk and I are just going to practise one last song.
   Gregory, do you know where the gin is?

Gregory You hum it, Queenie, and I'll play it.

Stella Night, Mum.

   She walks up to bed.
   Lights down.

SIX

The next morning.
   Beattie and Mrs McGeever, ridiculously dolled up.
   Rushing around.

Mrs McGeever The big producer's coming. The big
producer's coming.
WE MUST BUFF. WE MUST BUFF.

Beattie Slow down, Mrs McGeever, I can't keep up.

Frank Cream enters.

Mrs McGeever BUFF THE MANAGER. BUFF THE
MANAGER.

Beattie It's best if you just – let her do it, sir.
It's over quicker.

Frank is buffed.

Mrs McGeever Washed. Wiped. Brushed. Polished.
Dusted.
Your tie.
It's squint. (*She fixes his tie.*)
There.

Beattie You look very smart, Mr Cream.

Frank Thank you, Beattie.

Mrs McGeever Shiny shiny shiny head.

Frank Thank you, Mrs McGeever.
Now. Everyone ready. Where's Queenie?

Beattie Don't know, sir.

Frank But she was so desperate to be here.

Gregory I think she may have had a little too much . . .
Dutch courage last night.

Frank Oh dear.

Gregory She may be . . . unwell this morning.

Mrs McGeever Flat on her so-called bad back more like.

Beattie Too late now. He's coming up the drive.

Mrs McGeever We've got enough to worry about without her putting her foot in it. She cannae sing.

Frank She sings beautifully.

Beattie and Mrs McGeever You fancy her.

Frank Here he is. The big producer.

Voices from off.

Lilian Slow down, Rico. Have you taken your pills?

Stanley He's taken his pills.

Now onstage.

Lilian No, Rico. It's not a dump. It's a nice quiet place.

Stanley Nobody'll bother you.

Lilian No work.

Stanley A holiday.

Lilian They have burgers.

Stanley They have golf.

Lilian They have everything you need.

Frank Welcome, welcome, Mr Manhattan.
Frank Cream.
Manager of the Grand.

The big producer doesn't shake Frank's hand.

I must say we're very pleased to have you here.

Stanley Can we have the key to our rooms, please?

Frank Of course.
The Excelsior Suite on the top floor. Excellent views over the Clyde. I'm sure it'll be just perfect for you. Beattie will show you to your room.
Beattie!

Mrs McGeever Do it. This is your chance.

Beattie I will.
Hello, Mr Manhattan . . .

*Beattie approaches them. Surreptitiously tap-dances
a moment.*

You're room's this way.

Frank Beattie?

Beattie Follow me.

Another weird little tap routine.

Stanley What're you . . .

Lilian She's . . .

Again she tap-dances to punctuate what she says.

Beattie Follow me. Top of the stairs. I'll take you up.

Lilian Mr Cream. Rico's identity was supposed to be top
secret!

Stanley Yes, Dad, she is tap-dancing.

Beattie I can do more . . .

And indeed she does.

Lilian I said NO AUDITIONS!

Frank I'm terribly sorry about this. Beattie!

Stanley He wants to dance.

Lilian Oh no.

Stanley He wants to show you how it's done.

Beattie Oh he does, does he?
I can show him a thing or two myself.

Stanley Is that a fact?

Beattie It certainly is.

Frank Beattie, don't be silly, you can't tap-dance.

Beattie Gregory!

Music starts.

PROVE IT!

THE TAP-DANCING SONG

Frank *and* **Gregory**
> Hey, the girl can really move it
> Just give our Scottish lass a chance to prove it

Lilian *and* **Stanley**
> He's better, he really knows the score

Frank *and* **Gregory**
> That crazy fat man's tearing up the floor
> Beattie, lassie, show him what to do
> Look at that, he didn't jump he flew

Lilian *and* **Stanley**
> Rico, baby, please don't go so mad
> That man ain't no fat man, that man he's my dad
>
> Give in you'll never beat him
> Give up you got no chance

Frank *and* **Gregory**
> He may be good, but he's made of wood
> You call that stomping 'dance'?
>
> Give in, you'll never beat her
> Give up, you're bound to lose

Lilian *and* **Stanley**
> She's a pretty miss but she can't do this
> He's so hot he melts his shoes

Frank *and* **Gregory**
> He's gonna burst

Lilian *and* **Stanley**
> Slow down, Rico
> She'll crack first

Frank *and* **Gregory**
> Go, Beattie, go
> She's got some inner vision
> Tap-dancing is her life

Lilian *and* **Stanley**
> He's got a heart condition
> I know, 'cos I'm his wife
>
> Give in you'll never beat him
> Give up you got no chance

Frank *and* **Gregory**
> He may be good, but he's made of wood
> You call that stomping 'dance'?
>
> Give in, you'll never beat her
> Give up, you're bound to lose

Lilian *and* **Stanley**
> She's a pretty miss but she can't do this
> He's so hot he melts his shoes

Frank *and* **Gregory**
> You know I used to do a bit of tap dancing myself.
> But I had to give it up.
> Why's that?
> I kept falling in the sink

Lilian *and* **Stanley**
> What's the cure for water on the brain?
> I dunno
> A tap on the head

Frank *and* **Gregory**
Stop them someone – they've gone ballistic

Lilian *and* **Stanley**
Stop them please before somebody dies

Frank *and* **Gregory**
Their supersonic pas de deux's unrealistic
They're maddened, crazy, desperate for the prize

Lilian *and* **Stanley**
Stop the music, oh my God, we must restrain them

Frank and Gregory
Look they've spoiled my lovely polished floor
Slap them, hit them, trip them, if necessary brain them

Lilian *and* **Stanley** The piano player's expired –

Frank and Gregory We won

Lilian *and* **Stanley** We won

Gregory The contest was a draw!

Stanley He can't get up.

Lilian We'll have to carry him upstairs.
Look what you've done to my Rico!

Frank Do enjoy your stay.

They carry the Big Producer up the stairs.

Frank Beattie. For goodness' sake.

Beattie Wow. What a great dancer.

Mrs McGeever You fancy him.

Beattie I think I maybe do.

Gregory No. I don't believe it.

Mrs McGeever Is he not awful small for you?

Beattie Size is of no importance to me, Mrs McGeever.

Gregory She's dumped me for Pinocchio. (*Leaves in a huff.*)

Frank Beattie. I insist. No more auditions for Mr Manhattan.
He's the most prestigious guest we've ever had at the Grand. And I don't want him upset. Is that clear? Now go and prepare the dining room for this afternoon.

Beattie Yes, sir. Sorry, sir.

Beattie and Mrs McGeever exit.

Frank Good.
DANNY! DANNY! LUGGAGE FOR YOU TO TAKE UPSTAIRS.

Stella and Queenie appear at the top of the stairs. Queenie in a terrible state.

Queenie Where were you?

Queenie (*in a whisper*) I've lost my voice.

Frank What? I can't hear you, Queenie.

Queenie (*in a whisper*) I've lost my voice.

Frank Sorry?

Stella She's lost her voice.

Gesture of despair from Queenie.

Gregory Something of a blessing in disguise.

Frank Oh no. Queenie. We'll . . . we'll think of something.
A doctor. We'll call a doctor.

Queenie I have a bit of a headache as well.

Frank What?

Stella She has a headache as well.

Frank My poor Queenie.
We'll sort something out.
We'll make sure you're able to sing for Mr Manhattan.

Danny arrives.

Danny Morning, all. Everyone's glum. Somebody died?

Frank Ms Trotter has lost her voice.

Danny Serves her right. Too much shouting. At Stellster here.

Frank Danny.

Stella She's desperate to audition for Mr Manhattan.
It's her big chance.
She wants to go to Hollywood.

Danny Hollywood. Schmollywood. Who cares?

Frank I'll call a voice doctor, Queenie, the best there is.

Gregory He'll need to be a blooming genius to fix her voice.

Stella Danny, you know you said, if there was ever anything I needed . . .

Danny Yes. 'S what I said. True as well.

Stella Well . . . I need . . . Mum needs to be able to sing.
It's important.
Really. Please. Can you fix it?

Danny You ask. It's done . . . Danny can sort it.
Everything's under control.
The lady.

Will sing.
For the big producer.

Frank But how?

Stella She can barely croak.

Gregory Even when she has got a voice.

Danny Don't worry.
Danny 306.
Has got a plan.

Lights down.

SEVEN

Later on that afternoon.
The Big Producer, Lilian and Stanley are going out
to play golf. Queenie, operated by Frank Cream and
Beattie, is lying on top of the piano with a mirror in her
hands. Gregory is playing foyer music.

Stanley The golf course here is the best there is, Dad.

Lilian You two promise to play gently.
Stanley, let your daddy win. I don't want him getting
upset.

Stanley Yes, Mom.

Lilian He likes to be the best on the course.

Stanley You certainly are, Dad. You're the best golfer
this side of LA.

Lilian Are you wearing your vest?
Have you got warm socks?
Don't stay out on the course too long . . .

Song begins. The Big Producer stops in his tracks.
Queenie performs the song holding a small hand
mirror and doing make-up.

I thought no more auditions.
Rico's in a delicate condition . . .

Stanley
No but listen . . .

SHE CAN'T BE ME

I walk down the High Street on Saturday
And I try to walk in a beautiful way
There's a face I can see in the glass
The face of the girl walking past
She's awkward and gawky and lost at sea
And I ask myself who can she be
Because she can't be me.

I see the girls with their gorgeous bobbed hair
Dancing around like they're floating on air
They are pretty and fashionably dressed
They're witty and so self-possessed
They laugh at the girl dancing so clumsily
You don't think they are laughing at me
No that couldn't be.

She's not me, you see
She just couldn't be
'Cos I can't be her and she can't be me
I'm the belle of the ball
The talk of the town
The most popular girl for miles around
Not a hair out of place
Not a mark on my face
All the joes and the beaus have the hots for me
Writers of musical shows write their plots for me
Who is this other girl downcast and blue?

Because she's got a face like the face of a girl I once
   knew.

If winter can turn into spring
And a river turn into the sea
And a promise turn into a lie
And a worm to a butterfly
And if history convinces
That frogs turn into princes
Then why can't, why can't I please . . .
Turn into me?

During the song, Stanley, suspicious, has discovered
Stella hidden behind a potted plant. The music stops.

Stanley Who are you?

Lilian She's sure got a voice.

The Producer beckons Stella over.

Come over here, baby.

Stella . . .

Lilian What's your name?

Stella . . .

Lilian She can sing, but she can't speak.

Stanley Whoever she is . . . she's a hundred times better
than that old croaker.

Queenie is dreadfully upset.

Stella Mum! I'm sorry.

Stella runs to Queenie. Queenie hurries upstairs,
embarrassed. Stella follows her, apologising. The door
slams.
   Lights down.

EIGHT

Later that day.
  Stanley is beside the kitchen hatch.

Stanley Chef? Chef?
  Mr Mayakovsky?

The hatch opens.

Mr Mayakovsky Go away.

Stanley I'm sorry, sir, but I wondered if . . .

Mr Mayakovsky I'm unhappy. I want to be alone.

Stanley Well, I'm sorry to hear that, sir.
  Maybe I'll come back later.

Mr Mayakovsky STAY THERE, BOY.
  I want to tell you something. (*He grabs Stanley's hand.*)
I have worked in the finest hotels of Europe.
  Kings and princes came into my kitchen and begged
to lick my icing bowl. I refused them. I was God. And
then . . . one little mistake . . . one tiny little chopping
accident . . . nothing . . . a petty little error . . . and I was
destroyed.

Stanley What happened, sir?

Mr Mayakovsky One of the kitchen boys ended up in
the stroganoff.
  A guest complained.
  It tasted good. What more do they want!
  Ungrateful shmuck.
  My career was in ruins. Nowhere would employ me.
And now look at me. I cook in this . . . rat hole . . . the
Grand Hotel, Cumdoon. Where nobody recognises my
true genius.

Stanley Sir. I do.

Mr Mayakovsky You do?

Stanley Sir. I've tasted burgers from LA to NYC. I've had flame-grill, char-grill, seared, braised, fried beef, ham, steak and chicken burgers. I've had every burger it's possible to imagine, sir, and I have never, never tasted a burger so fine as the one you made for me today. The one you called . . . Macdonald's.

Mr Mayakovsky You liked it?

Stanley Sir. I worshipped it.

Mr Mayakovsky Well, it's just a little someone – something – I threw together.

Stanley In fact, I came to ask if you would make one for my father.
    He's hungry right now.

Mr Mayakovsky I don't know if I have the right ingredients.
    Let me see.
    Oh yes . . . still an arm or two left.
    I can make you another one.
    Just one moment.

Stanley I'll wait.

Shouts from upstairs.

Queenie Get out! Get out! My life's ruined. Get out!
    Get somebody to get me a gin and go! I never want to see your ugly face again.

Stella emerges from her room. Very upset. She runs down the stairs. She bumps into Stanley.

Stanley Hey . . . slow down. You're upset.

Stella Let go.

Stanley lets go.

Stanley Sounds like your mom got her voice back.
And some.

Stella Leave me alone.

Stanley What is it with this country?. Everyone wants to be left alone.
What are y'all, Greta Garbo? I'm an American . . . we're friendly. Were not used to this kind of treatment.

Stella This is all your fault.

Stanley What is?

Stella If it wasn't for your stupid dad then none of this would have ever happened. Mum would be – just normal.

Stanley Seems to me your mom isn't normal, normally.

Stella You don't know anything.
You're just a big dumb . . . Yank!

Stanley I plead guilty.
I'm sorry.
Listen. Please. Don't be angry with me . . . I'm . . .
I'm an expert in dysfunctional parents myself.
My mom's from New York and my dad's only six inches tall.
It's a showbiz family.
Just like yours.
Sit down.
I'm waiting for the crazy Russian guy to make me a burger.
Maybe we can talk.

Stella sits down.

Stanley But only if you promise to be nice to me.
I'm only a big dumb Yank after all.
You promise?

Stella No. Maybe.

Stanley Maybe's good enough.
So what's the problem?

Stella Today was my mum's big chance. And I ruined it.
Now she hates me.

Stanley But listen to me. You've got talent. My dad was
impressed. He said he wanted you for his next picture.
You're something special.

Stella I don't want to be special. I just want to . . . be
normal.

Stanley You want to – go to school. See other kids.
Hang out.

Stella Yes.

Stanley You want to go home and Mom's cooked a big
apple pie or something.

Stella Yes. Well, you know, a scone, in my case.

Stanley You want to get help with your homework. You
want to be taken to see your grandparents at the
weekend.

Stella How do you know all this?

Stanley I told you. I'm an expert. Listen, I never see my
dad, he works all the time. He shoots movies. He goes to
movie parties.
He hangs out with movie-star buddies. And my mom.
She spends all her time making sure Pops doesn't have
a heart attack or something. All I know's being dragged

around film sets. I used to think that was how all kids grew up.

Stella Better than being dragged round hotels.

Stanley Maybe. Maybe it's just the same.

I know what it's like. But believe me. You think your life ain't normal but – this is something you find out in Hollywood – it ain't normal to be normal. Deep down, everybody's just some kind of freaky kid. And those freaky kids are the ones who grow up to be parents. So the way I see it. It's normal to have freaky parents and it's freaky to have normal ones.

Stella Do you think so?

Stanley I know so.

The chef's hatch opens.

Mr Mayakovsky One Macdonald's, right up. Would you like large fries?

Stanley What are fries?

Mr Mayakovsky It's a new idea. I was making the burger. Chopping, chopping, and when I start to chop, I just can't stop . . . I ended up chopping potatoes into small pieces and I just went crazy and threw them in the pan.

Stella Fried potatoes? Urgh.

Stanley tries one.

Stanley Hey . . . Mr Mayakovsky . . . these 'fries' are delicious. I love them.

Can I have something to drink with this?

Mr Mayakovsky Let me see, what have I got? . . . Some bleach, some old oil, aha . . . here . . . I have some old carpet cleaner . . . he'll never notice . . .

Here . . .

Stanley drinks some.

Stanley This is great. I've never tasted it before. What do you call it?

Mr Mayakovsky I don't know. I'm not a bartender. I'm only a cook.

Stanley Sorry?

Mr Mayakovsky I said I'm only a cook.

Stanley This guy's accent! Gee.

Mr Mayakovsky A COOK!

Stanley Coke! That's what he calls it. A Macdonald's. Fries and a coke.
   The food of the gods.

Mr Mayakovsky Americans . . . who understands them?

The kitchen hatch shuts.

Stanley Want some?

Stella No, thanks. It looks horrible.

Stanley Stella, it was really great to meet you.
   You should think about coming back to the States with us.
   How'd you like to be a star?

Stella Me?
   Nobody'd want to go the pictures to see me.

Stanley I would.

Queenie shouts from off.

Queenie OH GOD. I'M NEVER GOING TO BE A STAR! NEVER.
   I'M NEVER GOING TO GET MY HANDPRINTS ON HOLLYWOOD BOULEVARD. NEVER GO TO

THE OSCARS. NEVER HAVE A SWIMMING POOL. NEVER. I CAN'T BEAR IT.

Stella I can't go to Hollywood.
I'm busy.

Stanley At least think about it.
Mom can arrange everything.
First class to New York.
See you later, Stella. Maybe?

Stella Maybe.

Stanley exits up the stairs.

Macdonald's? Gee.

Gregory enters.
He sits at the piano.
He plays a recognisably sad tune.
He stops.
He sighs.
Stella and Frank sigh.

Gregory What am I? A simple musician, a tickler of ivories, a mere servant of Lady Jazz and Lord Honky-Tonk. Not much of a catch for a lady, I know, but I had a sweetheart, a girl I held a candle for . . . and now . . . She's shunned me and fallen in love with a tap-dancing American gnome. Life! One wonders why one bothers.

He plays the sad tune again.
Beattie enters, whistling a happy tune.
She double-takes the scene of melancholy.
Stella and Gregory sigh.

Beattie Oh God.
What a scene . . .
Who stole your scone?

Stella My mum hates me.

Beattie What about you?

Gregory Nothing.

Beattie C'mon . . . there must be something . . .

Gregory No. I'm fine.

All sigh.

Stella *and* **Gregory** Life!

Beattie Gregory.
I was thinking we could go out dancing tonight.
Do you fancy it?

Gregory Shouldn't you be off gallivanting with your pot-bellied midget fancy man.

Beattie Oh, that's what it is. You're jealous . . .

Gregory No.

Beattie Aye, y'are.

Gregory Nothing you can say will placate me, Beattie.
How can I come dancing with you? You think I'm a flop.

Beattie No, I don't, I think you're the bee's knees.

Gregory You think I'm a bore.

Beattie I think you're the cat's pyjamas.

Gregory You think I'm . . . I'm . . .

Beattie I think you're grand.

Gregory Really.

Beattie Really . . .

BABY YOU'RE JUST GRAND

If you're ever feeling down and in the dumps
If you ever feel like you're the king of chumps
All you need's a friend to hold your hand
Someone to tell you, 'Baby, you're just grand!'

So meet me down the high street half past eight
Get dressed up in your best and don't be late
And we'll go dancing till we cannae stand.
I will tell you, 'Baby, you're just grand!'

Beattie *and* **Gregory**
So when you think
Life is a chore
And nobody loves you any more
Come and stay at the Grand
That's where I'll be
Check in at reception here's your key . . .

Frank Cream enters.

Frank Stella! How's your mother?

Stella I don't know. She won't talk to me.

Frank Oh.

Stella Yes. Oh.

Frank You know, Stella, your mother's a wonderful woman.

Stella Sometimes.

Frank I remember so clearly the first time I saw her.
   I was in London, staying at the Ritz, checking out the competition, you know . . . I think the Grand came out of it very well . . . but that's by the by. The point is, the moment she came onstage to sing I . . . I . . . was . . . lost. In a dream.

Her . . . presence . . . Stella, she just seemed so . . . alive.
And ever since then I've struggled to get her booked
for a season at the Grand. Year after year she turned me
down.
But finally, this year, she said yes.

Stella We were desperate.

Frank What?

Stella We were . . . desperate to come here.

Queenie I HATE YOU ALL. I HATE THIS PLACE.
I HATE LIFE.

Stella She's not happy.

Frank Let me deal with this, Stella.
I refuse to allow anyone to be unhappy at the Grand.
Least of all my star.

Frank goes upstairs.

Frank
Queenie, do forgive me shouting from the stair
But I really couldn't stand to hear you in despair
I know your show has recently been panned
But Queenie, darlin', I think you're just grand.

All
So if it seems
That life is cruel
Here's an exception that proves the rule
Come to the Grand
That's where I'll be
Check in at reception here's your key . . .

Frank enters Queenie's room.
Danny enters.

Danny Da broad was looking blue.

I walked in. I said. Baby – best cure I know for da blues. 'S a gobstopper. Only half-sucked.

Stella Thanks.

Danny Plan didn't. Go to plan. Sorry.

Stella Not your fault.

Danny That sneaky. Snoopy. Slimy. Yank got the better of me.
I should've known.
He looks like a sneak. He looks like a snoop. He's got specs.

Stella He's alright. I talked to him.

Danny Watch out for speccies. That's what I say. Don't trust 'em.
Whatcha doing later?

Stella Nothing.

Danny Got to cheer you up. Stella. Raise a smile.
Let's go to the beach.

Stella I don't know. I don't feel in the mood for smiling.

Danny C'mon. Danny knows best. Follow me.

> Take off your shoes I'll take you to the sea
> We'll jump the waves and maybe you'll give me
> A stick to write our names with in the sand
> And I will show you just how life is grand.

Danny Promise you'll come?

Stella Promise.

All
> Some people say
> That life's a bore
> But I don't listen any more

'Cos I live at the Grand
And that's where I'll be
Check in at reception here's your key.

Life is grand at the Grand
We welcome everyone
If you're think you're a freak
If you're Belgian French or Greek.

We understand at the Grand
The only rule is fun
It's a place that's unique
It's quite simply *fantastique*.

*Frank Cream and Queenie have appeared at the top
of the stairs.*

Frank
You had a dream of stardom now you feel excluded
But Greta Garbo never made me smile like you did
Hollywood don't want you but on the other hand
You're the leading lady at the Grand.

Beattie
So when you think
Life is a chore
And nobody loves you any more
There's a seaside hotel
That's where I'll be
Check in at reception here's your key . . .

Frank Stella . . . I think your mother . . . wants to talk
to you.

*Queenie appears, shamefaced. She and Frank come
downstairs.*

Go on. Say what you said to me.
She's embarrassed.
Go on.

Stella It doesn't matter . . .

Frank No . . . Queenie . . .

Queenie is passed to Stella.

Queenie I'm sorry.

Stella No, it's my fault. I'm sorry.

Queenie No it's my fault. I'm sorry . . .

Stella No, it's . . .

Queenie Darling, do let me finish. I was wrong. I was angry with you because I was jealous. That's all . . .

Stella Jealous of what? Me? I'm an ugly mouse. You're a star, Mum, a performer.

Queenie Darling, I'm a dreadful old croaker.
You're the one who can sing.

Stella They've asked me to go to Hollywood.
They want me to be in a film.

Queenie Do you want to go?

Stella Yes.

Queenie Well, you must go then.

Stella I can't.

Queenie Why not?

Stella Because . . . because . . .
Well . . . who'd look after you?

Frank takes Queenie.

Frank I don't think you need to worry about your mother, Stella.

Stella Why not?

Queenie Tell her, Frank.

Frank She has graciously agreed to . . . marry me.

Stella You?

Queenie Well, he was available and – I'm no spring chicken.

Frank Queenie will be a permanent fixture at the Grand!

Queenie Just like the carpets. A bit tatty, a bit faded, but still essentially the *crème de la crème*.

Frank The cream de la cream.

Queenie Now. I want you to get yourself packed and ready.
We've got a lot to get done before you go.
You have to learn how to be a star.

Stella Me – I don't know how to do all that stuff.

Queenie Darling, it's all an act. Anyone can learn it. It just takes practice.
A little practice, petal, and you'll be just like me. Now Frank and I have a little celebrating of our own to do.

Frank and Queenie exit.

Stella But . . .

Queenie Not too much tonic for me, Frank darling . . . it gives me a headache.

Stella I don't want to be like you.
I don't ever want to end up.
Like you.

Lights down.

TEN

The next morning.
  Danny waiting for Stella.
  He waits. He waits.

Danny Stella! Stellie? Stellster!
  Said she'd be here.
  Rat. Bat. Traitor.
  I hate her.

  Beattie and Mrs McGeever enter.

Beattie What's wrong, Danny?

Danny Nothing. 'S fine. I'm okay.

Beattie You seem awfy sad.

Mrs McGeever He seems awfy mucky. And what do we
do with mucky boys!
  Beattie!

  They half-buff, half-tickle him.

Danny Get off. Go away. Leave me alone.

  They stop.

Beattie We were only messing. Only mucking about.
  Cheer up.

Danny I don't want to cheer up. I'm going off. I'm going
to the beach. (*Danny exits.*)

Beattie What's up with him.

Mrs McGeever Beattie. I've seen it before. And I'll see
it again.
  That is one of nature's most terrifying sights.
  It's worse than a tidal wave. It's worse than a hurricane.
  That is a boy with the big humpf about a lassie.

Queenie, Frank and Stella arrive from a shopping trip.
They are laden with bags and packages.
Stella looks gorgeous, transformed, a star.

Frank I just have one last little present I've organised.
I won't be a moment.

Beattie Wow, Stella, you look – brilliant!

Stella Do I?

Frank Beattie! In my office. There's a present for the
ladies.

Beattie and Mrs McGeever exit.

Queenie Darling . . .
You're doing it all wrong.
When someone pays you a compliment.
Don't blush. You say . . .

Queenie shows her.

'Why, thank you, you're so kind.'
Try it.

Stella (*mumbled*) Thank you, you're so kind.

Queenie Don't mumble. Do it again.

Stella Thank you. You're so kind.

Beattie re-enters heaving a bucket of wet concrete.

Frank Tah dah!
For my two favourite women . . .

Queenie What's that?

Frank This, Queenie, is a bucket of wet concrete.

Queenie How delightful.
Most men give their fiancées a ring.
Mine gives me building materials.

Stella What's it for?

Frank pours it onto the floor.

Queenie Good God, he's lost his mind.

Frank If you can't get to Hollywood Boulevard,
Queenie, then I insist that Hollywood Boulevard comes
to you.
I want you to print your hands in this concrete and
we'll embed it in the foyer . . .
In honour of Queenie and Stella . . . the stars of the
Grand.
The Queens of Cumdoon.

Queenie Frank, you're such a honey. Isn't he a honey?
Now. Stella, watch this, this can be the first lesson.

*With consummate professionalism, Queenie imprints
her hands into the concrete.*

Copy me.

Queenie walks, Stella walks with her.

Good, good, darling.
Lesson two.
The star thanks her fans for being so supportive.

*Queenie quiets an audience of adoring fans, feigns
shyness . . .*

Do it with me, darling.

Hoarse voice.

Thank you. Thank you so much, ladies and gen'lemen.
You've been a lovely audience.
You mean so much to me.
Truly.

Stella I can't say that.

Queenie Yes you can . . .
   Try.

Stella Thank you . . .

Queenie Humble, darling. Humble!

Stella Thank you so much, ladies and gentlemen.

Queenie Love. You love them.

Stella You've been a lovely audience.

Queenie Nearly crying! You're nearly crying. Choke back the tears.

Stella It means so much to me.

Queenie Excellent, excellent. We'll soon have you whipped into shape.

   Stella puts her handprints into the concrete.
      Stanley has appeared. He watches her.

Stella Thank you. Thank you so much.
   You're a lovely audience . . .
   You . . .
   This isn't me.
   I don't believe it.
   You should do this, not me.

Queenie It may surprise you to know this, but I used to be like you, Stella. I was good but I was shy. I didn't believe. When I got out there in front of all those people I suddenly felt as though I was . . . made of wood. So, do you know what I did? Just before I went onstage, I'd have a little gin, just to calm my nerves. So every night a little gin, and then a bigger one and then . . . darling, it wasn't really me out there, it was a bottle of gin and a body. And people noticed. And the audience got smaller. And the bookings got fewer and then . . . well, here we are. Because I didn't believe. You sang yesterday. Stella. It's your big chance, don't throw it away. I lost my chance years ago.

Now, you don't want to end up like . . . me. Do you?

Frank exits with Queenie.

Queenie Frank, darling, you do know how to charm a girl . . .

Concrete.

Really.

You're so romantic.

Frank Together, Queenie, we'll make a success of this place.

I know it.

Queenie Sometimes all a girl needs is a well-stocked bar and an adoring fan. I feel at home already.

Stella looks around her at the starry clothes and the packages. She doesn't seem happy.

STAR

Stella

I can't do it
I can't be a star
Don't have the words
The clothes, the looks
Don't have the car
To sing in front of people
And not know who they are
I can't do it
I just can't be a star
Star . . . star . . . star . . .

Stanley

    No doubt about it
    She's gonna be a hit
    That thing that 'it' girls have
    This girl she sure has it
    She's got that continental thing
    They call *je ne sais quoi*
    I just know it
    She's gonna be a star
    Star . . . star . . . star . . .

Stella

    A star's a million million miles away
    'Cross galaxies, across the Milky Way
    I never thought that I would be
    The kind of person people want to see
    Shining from a stage so far away
    Someone people dream of meeting
    On some special day.

Stanley

    She can do it
    She's got the future in her hands
    Marlene Dietrich better make
    Some other plans
    She's beautiful, she's gorgeous
    She's bound to wow the fans
    She can do it, the future's in her hands.

Stella

    Look at me

Stanley

    Look at her

Stella

    I'm so plain

Stanley
    She's amazing.
    She's beautiful

Stella
    I wish I were

Stanley
    Of course you are
    I can't stop gazing

Stella
    Can I do it
    Be a celebrity
    Read stories, scandals
    Gossip columns about me
    I'm just a girl, I don't know the world
    Of high society
    Can I do it? Could that star be me?
    Me . . . me . . . me . . .

Stella *and* **Stanley**
    Star . . . star . . . star . . .

    Danny has been watching.
        Stanley applauds.

Stella Thank you very much.
    You've been a lovely audience.
    It means a lot to me.
    Truly.

Stanley Are you packed and ready?
    We're leaving tomorrow.
    The liner sails for New York.
    You'll be there, right?

Stella I . . .

Stanley See you tomorrow, right?
    Right.

She has seen Danny.
Stanley exits.

Stella Danny.

Danny That's me. That's what my friends call me. You can call me Mr 306. Since you're not my friend.

Stella Yes I am.

Danny Don't think so.
Don't think I make friends with – grown-ups.
(*mocking*) Thenkyew very mich, yew've been a levly audience.
No.
Don't think so.

Stella I couldn't come to the beach . . . Frank and my mum . . .

Danny Don't want to hear. Excuses. Not listening.
Had a high old time.
By myself. Best company there is.
Counted clouds. Skimmed stones in the sea. Got six bounces off one. Saw a sunset. You wouldn't have liked it.
You still here?
Shouldn't you be in the USA.

Stella Maybe I should.

Danny Don't care either way.

Stella Well neither do I, then.

Danny Always thought you were stuck up anyway.

Stella Always thought you were . . . immature.

Danny Probably best you go, then.

Stella Probably best I do.

Danny Glad to see the back of you.

Stella Glad to see the back of you.

Danny You're making a mistake. You'll be disappointed. Know why?
You're not good enough.

Stella You think so?

Danny I'm telling you.

Stella Telling me?
Well, that's a shame, Danny 306, because I don't have nobody telling me what to do. Not any more. Understand?

Stella exits.
Danny is furious with himself.
Beattie and Mrs McGeever appear. They watch – in horror.

Danny Nobody sticks by Danny. Everybody moves on.
Friends come. Friends go. Don't need no one.
Look after myself. Look after myself alright.

Danny collapses. Sobbing.
Beattie and Mrs McGeever approach Danny and comfort him.
Stella, unseen, has come back. She watches.

Mrs McGeever Danny.
What are you playing at, you daft laddie?

Danny I thought she was a friend.

Mrs McGeever Of course she's your friend. You numpty.
But she won't be if you carry on like this.
Trying to stop her doing what she's good at. The thing she wants to do.

Danny Why doesn't she just stay here – the Grand's good enough for me. Why isn't it good enough for her?

Mrs McGeever You belong here, Danny. It's your place.
Stella's a visitor.
She's got other places she's got to go to.
Doesn't mean she won't come back.

Danny I don't want her to go.

Mrs McGeever Take a lesson from me.
Look at my Tommy.
You wouldn't think it to look at him.
But my Tommy was once a man of action.
A few years ago.
He had a dream.
He stirred in his seat. He kicked off his slippers.
He put down his garibaldi and he gave me a look full
of passion.
And he said to me, 'Muriel! I want to travel up the
Amazon in a canoe.
I feel it is my destiny.'
But I wouldn't let him.
I said, 'Tommy, if you go up that Amazon, you'll just
come back mucky.' So I said no.
And ever since then. He's been like this.
Hardly moves from his armchair.
Look. You can poke him with a stick. He won't
budge.
He's a broken shell of a man.
Now, Danny, could you do that to Stella?

Danny No.

Mrs McGeever There you go.

Danny She'll go to America and she'll forget about me.

Danny goes to exit.

Mrs McGeever No, she won't.

Danny How d'you know?

Mrs McGeever People don't forget the Grand, Danny.
Even if they try.
People never forget it.

Danny exits.

Beattie Is that a true story, Mrs McGeever, about you
denying your Tommy his destiny?

Mrs McGeever Ach no, Beattie. Look at him. He's a wee
dumpling and I love him. But the closest that man's been
to adventure's a trip on the Rothesay ferry – and even
that brought him out in a rash.

They exit.
*Stella comes down the stairs again to the wet
concrete. She kneels down and writes something in the
concrete.*

ELEVEN

The next morning.
Stanley at the kitchen hatch.

Mr Mayakovsky How may I help you?

Stanley One Macdonald's with fries and a coke please.

Mr Mayakovsky Certainly, sir.
Would you like to go large with that?

Stanley Yes, please.

Mr Mayakovsky Coming right up.

Stanley You know, Mr Mayakovsky, I like your burgers
so much I . . . well, I've been thinking, maybe you'd like
to come to America with me. I believe we could make a
business out of your burgers.

Mr Mayakovsky Oh.

Stanley What's the problem?

Mr Mayakovsky Well, Stanley, my friend, the problem is really ingredients.

Stanley You can't get them in America?

Mr Mayakovsky Do you have an endless supply of spotty, spectacled, teenage boys in America?

Stanley I think so.

Mr Mayakovsky That's what I need to make my burgers.

Stanley Oh! You mean to serve the customers. Like kitchen boys.

Mr Mayakovsky Exactly. Like the kitchen boy I . . . used to have.

Stanley What a great idea . . . we wouldn't have to pay waiters.
  We could use them to serve at the counters.

Mr Mayakovsky They wouldn't . . . stay in the job for very long.

Stanley No problem . . . I think this could be a whole new concept.
  Spotty speccy teenagers, serving customers these Macdonald's . . . and cokes and fries . . . yes . . . I think this could take off . . .

Mr Mayakovsky Very spotty. Very oily. Helps the flavour.

Stanley Yeah. Mr Mayakovsky. You got a deal.

  Lilian enters.

Lilian RICO! RICO! Where's your father, Stanley? I can't find him.
The poor man's got a heart condition.

Beattie and Mrs McGeever enter, at speed.

Mrs McGeever NO MUCK. ALL CLEAN. ALL MUST BE CLEAN.

Lilian My God! It's Godzilla!

Mrs McGeever MUCK ON MY FLOOR. MUST BE REMOVED. MUST BE SHINY. MUST BE BUFFED.

Lilian Help! Help! Stanley!

Beattie switches her alarm.

Mrs McGeever Cup of tea. Cup of tea. Cup of tea.

Beattie Sorry about that.
She's a bit neurotic about her clean floors.
She'll basically destroy anything that gets in her way.

Lilian It's a terrifying sight.

Beattie It's very normal in Scotland.

Lilian I'm glad I'm leaving. Now, have you seen my husband? I can't find him anywhere.

Beattie Oh.

Lilian What do you mean . . . oh?

Beattie Well, he wouldn't have been . . . on the floor, would he?

Lilian Well of course he would. He can't fly.

Beattie Oh.
Oh dear.
You shouldn't have left him on the floor.
A wee fellow like that. He didn't stand a chance.

Lilian What are you saying!

Beattie I'm terribly sorry, missis –

Beattie empties out the Hoover bag. Amongst the detritus, Rico.

Lilian My God, is he alive?

Stanley Dad!

Rico, gets up, dusts himself off. Does a quick tap dance.

What did you say, Dad?

Lilian He said – he'd never felt better,

Stanley He said – he felt brand new.

Mrs McGeever He would.
That's what it feels like.
When you've been given a right good buffing.

Lilian Where's the girl? I thought she was coming with us.
Rico's booked recording studios and everything.

Stanley She's not here yet.

Lilian We haven't got time to hang around.
Is she coming or is she not coming?

Frank, Queenie and Stella arrive. Stella has a suitcase.

At last. She's here. Now we can go.

Queenie Good luck, darling. Break a leg. Write to us.

Frank You'll be a big hit. I know it.

Stella I can't find Danny anywhere.

Queenie But darling, they'll leave without you.

Stella I can't go.

Lilian Come on, honey. There's a ship waiting for us.

Stella I can't until I've said goodbye to him.

Stanley We have to hurry.

Stella DANNY! DANNY!

Beattie He's sulking.
He says he doesn't want to see you.

The sound of a ship's horn hooting.

Lilian That's our boat. It's parked just outside.

Frank If you're going – you have to go now.

Stella . . .

Queenie Well Darling . . . what do you say?

TRAVEL LIGHT

Stella
I've never been the kind of girl to stay long in one
  spot
Never had a house and garden like some kids have got
I couldn't count the beds I've slept in, so many I forgot
But I like hotels, you feel at home, even when you're
  not.

All
When you leave, take only what you need
A change of underwear
And your memories
Travel light, 'cos you'll be moving on
And one day everything but memories are gone.

Stella
Everything's the start of something, everything's
  the end
One day you make an enemy the next you make
  a friend

Just make sure to keep addresses for the postcards
   that you'll send
You say goodbye in one place, say hello the other end.

All

When you leave, take only what you need
A change of underwear
And your memories
Travel light, 'cos you'll be moving on
And one day everything but memories are gone.

We'll think of you, we'll look out for your name
   in lights
You could paper China with all the letters that
   we'll write
If you ever need a pal who's handy in a fight
Then telegram, or phone us, we'll make sure that
   you're alright.

Be good, now
Make sure and eat your greens
Dress warm
Just be polite
Stay down to earth
Remember us
Don't stay out late at night
If you're feeling blue
Remember
This'll always be your place
Can I just lick a tissue,
And wipe around your face?
When you leave, take only what you need
A change of underwear
And your memories.

Travel light, 'cos you'll be moving on
And one day everything but memories are gone.

Stella

> I wonder what it will be like, the next time I come
> back?
> Will Danny still be playing tricks, will Beattie get
> the sack?
> Will Mr Mayakovsky still plan serial attacks?
> Will Gregory play piano, or will he have lost the
> knack?

All

> When you leave, take only what you need
> A change of underwear
> And your memories
> Travel light, 'cos you'll be moving on
> And one day everything but memories are gone.

A ship's horn toots again.

Stanley Come on, Stella. We've gotta go.

Stella DANNY. ARE YOU THERE. DANNY?

Lilian Send the kid a postcard.

Stanley and Lilian leave.

Mrs McGeever Beattie. That boy Danny should be here.

Beattie He's in a huff.

Mrs McGeever Well let's buff his huff.

Stella

> No point looking far ahead, who knows where we'll
> all be
> Who knows what we'll be doing when nearly ninety-
> three
> All I know is you will still be you and I will still be me
> And I know I won't forget you, you meant everything
> to me.

Tell Danny I'll never forget him.
    Tell him I'll never forget the Grand.

Gregory I think I'm going to cry.

Stella leaves.
    Beattie and Mrs McGeever enter dragging Danny.

Mrs McGeever What does it take to talk some sense into you, lad?

Danny Ow. Ooyah. My ear.

Beattie She's gone. Oh no. We've missed her.

Mrs McGeever Danny. Look what she wrote . . .

They show Danny the concrete.

Danny Danny. 306. + Me. For ever.

Mrs McGeever Isn't that nice?

Danny Suppose.

Mrs McGeever So.

Beattie The boat's going.

Danny climbs up to the window to see the boat.

Danny Umph gumph glub flub. Stella.

All What?

Danny Umph gumph. Glub flub.

Frank What does that mean?

Danny She'll understand.

All
    When you leave, take only what you need
    A change of underwear
    And your memories

Travel light, 'cos you'll be moving on
And one day everything but memories are gone.

TWELVE

*Old Stella, scrabbling in the dust to find her graffito in
the concrete.*
   A car horn tooting outside.
   Andy, Sandi and Mandi enter.

Andy You still here, Miss Stella?

Sandi We were tooting the car horn.

Mandi She's a bit deaf.

Andy This place bring back a few memories?

Sandi I can't imagine what it must have been like in the
olden days.

Mandi Hey, look over here, there's a record player.

   They go over and look.
   *They find all Stella's records and even posters of
her.*

Andy Wow! What a collection.

Sandi Somebody must have been a big fan of yours.

Mandi Somebody must have collected these things for . . .
it's your entire career.

Andy I'd love to listen to one of those . . .

   He puts one on the record player.
   Stella's song plays.

Stella (*crackly on a seventy-eight*)
   I walk down the high street on Saturday

And I try to walk in a beautiful way
There's a face I can see the glass
The face of the girl walking past
She's awkward and gawky and its plain to see
She can't be me.

I see girls with their gorgeous bobbed hair
Dancing past like they're walking on air
They're so pretty, their dress sense
So witty, such confidence
And they laugh at the girl dancing clumsily
Well, it can't be me

I'm not me, you see, I just couldn't be
I can't be her and she can't be me
I'm the belle of the ball, I'm the talk of the town
The most popular girl for miles around
Not a hair out of place not a plook on my face
All the beaus and the joes have their eyes on me
I've even got a first-class college degree
So who's she?
She can't be me.

Stella dances. Danny enters. Old. They dance together.

In the movies a girl dates a guy
With a dangerous look in his eye
He's handsome and charming
Polite and disarming
He'd never date that dull girl, you see
He'd date me.

Not me, you see, she just couldn't be
I can't be her and she can't be me
I'm the belle of the ball, I'm the talk of the town
The most popular girl for miles around
Not a hair out of place not a plook on my face
All the beaus and the joes have their eyes on me

I've even got a first-class college degree
So who's she?
She can't be me.

If winter can turn into spring
And a river turn into the sea
If promises turn into lies
And caterpillars turn into butterflies
And if history convinces
That frogs turn to princes
Then why can't I turn into me?
Why can't I turn into me?

I'm not me, you see, I just couldn't be
I can't be her and she can't be me
I'm the belle of the ball, I'm the talk of the town
The most popular girl for miles around
Not a hair out of place not a plook on my face
All the beaus and the joes have their eyes on me
I've even got a first-class college degree
So who's she?
She can't be me.

The End.

STEPPING STONES

Mike Kenny

*a play for young people with learning disabilities
and their families and friends*

Stepping Stones was first performed on 5 February 1997 by Interplay Theatre Company at Ganton School, Hull. The cast was as follows:

Cynth Karen Spicer
Mam Caroline Parker
Monty, Flint, Man Garry Robson
Musician Nick Cattermole

Director Jenny Sealey
Designer Lisa Ducie
MD Sam Paechter

Characters

Cynth

Mam

Monty

Flint

Man

The stars in the sky.
They seem to have always been.
Suddenly one moves.

Cynth
Mam! Mam! Mam!
That. That. That.
What's that?

Mam
What?

Cynth
That.
Up there.

Mam
Oh that.
Nothing.

Cynth
Nothing?

Mam
Nothing.

Cynth
Nothing's beautiful.
It looks like something to me.
Beautiful nothing.

Mam
It's a star. A star.

Now go back to sleep, Cynth, please.
Just a falling star.

Cynth
Thanks, Mam.
Mam. Mam. Mam.

Mam
What?

Cynth
Tonight a star dropped
Other side of the mountain.
Can I look for it?

Mam
Don't be silly, Cynth.
Go back to sleep.

Dawn. Spring. Windy.

Dawn is rising. Slowly. Cynth is sitting watching it,
eating. Mam is busy, hanging out washing. Occasionally
Cynth drops something. Mam picks it up, sometimes
before it even touches the floor. Mam puts food in
Cynth's mouth. Cynth is singing and rocking. Loud.

Cynth
Sun. Sun. Sun.
Sun on the mountain.
Sunshine comes up. Come up sun.
Sunshine come up sun.

It's a windy day.
Mam is hanging out washing.
It all points one way.

The wind is blowing very strongly one way, so that it nearly blows everything over. It's easy to go one way, but a real battle to go the other.

Mam
A good drying day.
Wind whips away the wetness.
The rain's somewhere else.

Cynth
Where?

Mam
Somewhere.

Cynth
Where?

Mam
Somewhere.
Somewhere else.
I don't care.

Cynth (*points*)
What's there?

Mam
What?

Cynth
What's there?

Mam
What?

Cynth
Over there. What's over there?

Mam
Where?

Cynth
Over the mountain. What's there? What's over there?

Mam
Nothing.

Cynth
Nothing?

Mam
Nothing.

Cynth
Nothing? Nothing? Nothing?
A hole?
Lots of holes.

Mam
No.
Just nothing. (*Beat.*) Much.

Cynth
How come?

Mam
How come what?

Cynth
How come nothing . . . much?

Mam
Just is.

Cynth
Just is?

Mam
Just is.

Cynth
Just is?

Just is?
How come?

Mam
How should I know?

Cynth
You're Mam. You're my mam. You know everything.

Mam
I haven't got the time to answer all your questions.

Cynth
Why not?

Mam
Too many. Too busy. Make yourself useful. Hold the
washing basket.

Cynth
I'm full of questions.
I'm like an empty basket.
Full of emptiness.
Nothing.
Got to fill it.
Stars up in the sky.
Sunshine on the mountain top.
Got to go. Somewhere.

Mam
What?

Cynth
Got to go.
Got to go.

Mam
Where?

Cynth
There. Over there. Over the mountain.

See what's what.
Got to go.

Mam
Go?!

Cynth
Go.
Go. Go. Go.

Mam
Go?
Why this sudden rush to go?

Cynth
Don't know.
Don't know.
Don't know the answer.
I ask questions.
You do answers.
Why this sudden rush to go?

Mam
I don't know.

Cynth
I want to go.

Mam
No.

Cynth
Let me go.

Mam
No.

Cynth
Please.

Mam
No. No.

Cynth
Yes. Yes. Yes. Yes. Yes.

Cynth falls asleep. Mam tidies and looks at her. Tense. Waits for her to wake. She does.

Yes. Yes. Yes.

Mam
No. No. No.

Cynth
Please.

Mam
No.

Cynth
Why not?

Mam
Because.

Cynth
Because?

Mam
Because.

Cynth
Because . . .

She falls off the end of it.

Mam
Because Mam says so.

Cynth
Because Mam says so?

Mam
Yes.

Cynth

Well Cynth says so. What?
Cynth says so what.

Mam

So what?

Cynth

So what.

Mam

So . . .
It's a big, big world out there.

Cynth

What's there?

Mam

I don't know. Nothing.

Cynth

Like me!
I don't know nothing neither.
Know nothing, never will.

Mam

The world's a scary place.
You know nothing.

Cynth

Whose fault's that?

Mam

One day.

Cynth

When?

Mam

Some day.

Cynth
When?

Mam
When you know something.

Cynth
What?

Mam
When you know what's what.

Cynth
What? When I know what's what?
When will I know what's what?

Mam
I know.
Have something nice to eat.

Cynth says nothing. Mam races off with the wind to get her something. Struggles back.

Cynth
Don't want that. (*Drops it.*)

Mam
I know.

She goes off to get something else. Cynth starts to pack things off the washing line. Secretly.

Mam (*returns*)
What about this? It's an apple off our tree.
I've kept it all winter

Cynth
Don't want that. (*Drops it.*)

Mam
You used to love it.

177

Cynth
Not now.

Mam
Why?

Cynth
People change, you know.

Mam (*catches Cynth packing*)
What are you doing?

Cynth
Going.

Mam
No.

Cynth
Yes.

Mam
Where?

Cynth
Don't know.
Somewhere.
Anywhere but here.

Mam
You want to leave home.
But what are you looking for?
Stay until you know.

Cynth
Stars up in the sky.
Sunshine on the mountain top.
Big big world out there.
Got to go.
Off to see what's what.

I'll know when I see it.
Don't try to stop me.

Mam
I'll help you.

Cynth
What?

Mam
I'll help you.
I'll help you pack.

Mam
You'll need to eat.
You'll need clothes to keep you warm
And clothes to keep you dry.
And something to remember this place (*a stone*)
So that you can find the way back.
And something to remember me by.

Cynth
I won't forget you.

Mam
You might.

Cynth
I won't. I won't.
Don't be silly.
You're my mam.
How could I forget my mam?
I'd always know you.
Goodbye.

She puts the backpack on.

Cynth
Mam.

Mam
  What?

Cynth
  I can't move.
  It's too heavy, I can't move.

Mam
  It's stuff you need.
  You'll need to eat.
  You'll need clothes to keep you warm
  And clothes to keep you dry.
  And something to remember this place
  So that you can find the way back.

Cynth
  But I can't go anywhere.
  Not like this.

Mam takes everything out and then climbs into the backpack.

  Mam.

Mam
  What?

Cynth
  What are you doing?

Mam
  Coming.

Cynth
  Where?

Mam
  With you.

Cynth doesn't speak.

Mam
You need me.

Cynth (*very quiet*)
No.

Mam
What?

Cynth
No.

Mam
Speak up.

Cynth
NO. NO. NO.

Mam
Don't you shout at me, young woman.

Cynth
You can't come with me.
I'm going on my own.
You can't come.
No.

Very quick packing. She takes a stone.

Mam (*very huffy, folding washing*)
Alright then. Suit yourself.

Cynth
I'm going away now.
Goodbye, Mam.

Sets off against the prevailing wind. Struggling, can't get anywhere.

Wind blows in my face.
On the day I left my home.
Go the other way.

Turns round and is blown away.

Mam
Take something.
Armsful of washing
Washed clean and dried by the wind.
Armsful. Heart empty.

She makes a decision. She follows Cynth.

Midday. Summer. Hot.
Sun blaze haze lazy daze.
Bees dose, no one plays.

Cynth (*arrives*)
Hot. Hot. Hot. Hot.
I'm here. I'm here
I got here. Here I am.
I'm here.
On my own.
I'm here on my own.
There's my house.
Little Little Little.
There it is.
Far away.
I'm here
On my own.

Monty
No you're not.
I'm here.

Cynth
How long have you been there?

Monty
Always.
As long as I can remember.

Cynth
Well, I'm here now too.

Monty
So
You're here then, are you?

Cynth
Yes.

Monty
And where's here then when it's at home?

Cynth
Oh no.
It's not home.
Home's there.
Over there.
Look.
You can see it.
Little house.

Monty
Yes.

Cynth
Little tree.

Monty
Yes.

Cynth
Little stream,

Monty
Yes.

Cynth
Little Mam.

Monty
No.
I can't see her.

Cynth
She's in the little house.
But I'm not there.
No this is here
And I came here on my own.

Does a dance.

I am here I am.
I used to be somewhere else.
Now I'm here I am.

Monty
Where you going now?

Cynth
Don't know.
I'm going to find out what's what.

Monty
Where?

Cynth
Don't know.
Somewhere else.

Falls asleep.

Monty
Hello? Hello?

She continues to sleep.

Mam (*arrives*)
Hot. Hot. Hot. Hot.

Monty
 Hello.

Mam
 Hello.

 She attacks Monty.

 What have you done to her?
 If you've touched her . . .
 So help me . . .
 I'll . . .

Cynth (*waking up*)
 Hello.
 Oh good, I'm still here.

 Mam hides.

 I thought I might have dreamed it all.
 I'm Cynth.

Monty
 I'm Monty.
 Monty Banks.

Cynth
 Pleased to meet you, Mr Banks.

Monty
 Likewise.

Cynth
 I'm here.

Monty
 So you said.

Cynth (*proudly and with great significance*)
 Without Mam.

185

Monty (*realising*)
I see. On your own!

Cynth
Yes.
I'm hungry.

Monty
Are you?

Cynth
Yes.

Mam, hearing this, digs in her bag and produces some food, puts it where Cynth can get it without seeing her. Cynth eats.

Monty
That looks nice.

Cynth
It is.

She carries on eating.

I'll be off soon.
Are you going anywhere?

Monty
No.

Cynth
Why not?

Monty
Can't find a good enough reason to go anywhere.
Where are you going?

Cynth
Don't know.

Monty
And why are you going there?

Cynth
I don't really know.
Saw a star drop from the sky
And felt like going.

Monty
I see.
Would you pass me that stone over there?

Cynth
Me?

Monty
Yes.

Cynth
Which one?

Monty
That one over there.

Cynth goes to where he is pointing. Monty reaches for the food that she has left near him.

Cynth
This one?

Monty
No. The other one.

Mam slaps his hand hard. He snatches it back.

Cynth (*returns with the stone*) Here it is.

Monty
Thanks.

He sniffs it as if savouring it.

Aaah lovely.

He pops it in a cooking pot.

Could you get me some water?

Cynth
Me?

Monty
From the river?

Cynth
Me?

Monty
If you'd be so kind.

Cynth
Me?

Monty
Well, there's nobody else about. Is there?

Cynth goes. Mam and Monty look daggers at one another.

Cynth (*returns*)
Here it is.

Monty
Thank you so much.

Cynth
Thirsty now.

Monty
There's water in the river.

Cynth
Where I live it's just a little stream.

Monty
Is that so?

Cynth
Yes, it is so.

Mam produces a drink and puts it within reach.
Cynth accepts this as perfectly normal.

Monty
And your mam stayed at home, did she?

Cynth
Oh yes, she went mad.
She didn't want me to come.
I came on my own.

Monty
I see.

Cynth
What you doing?

Monty
Lunch.

Cynth
What you having?

Monty
Soup.

Cynth (*looks in the pot*)
Stone soup? Funny lunch.

Monty
Delicious. Of course you need to know the right sort
of stone.

Cynth
I'm going, me.

Monty
Where?

Cynth
I don't know.

Monty
That way's nice.

Cynth
See you then.

She goes. Mam emerges from hiding.

Monty
I should just wait if I were you.

Mam
Why?

Monty
That way's nice, but it doesn't go anywhere.
Do you happen to have a carrot in there?

Mam
What if I have?

Monty
Well there's nothing like it for bringing out the flavour
of these stones.

Mam
Here.

Monty
Thanks.

Mam
You're welcome.

Monty
Monty.

Mam
Cynth's mam.

Cynth races in. Mam hides.

Cynth
That way was nice but it doesn't go anywhere.

Monty
Try that one.

Cynth
I will.

Monty
Before you go –

Cynth
Me?

Monty
Yes.
Have you got an onion in that bag of yours?

Cynth (*she looks*)
Yes.

Off she goes.

Monty (*to Mam*)
Have you got an onion?

Mam
Not for you.

She begins to follow Cynth.

Monty
That doesn't go anywhere either.

Mam
How do you know?

Monty
I've been there, you see.

I've travelled the world over.
Are you a great traveller?

Mam
What's it to you?

Monty
Just chit-chat.

Mam
Chit-chat?
Can't stand chit-chat.

*Cynth races in. Monty points another way. Cynth
nods and races off.*

Monty
Made no great journeys, then?

Mam
I might have
But I can't see that it's any of your business.

Monty
Suit yourself.
She your daughter, then?

Mam
I'm her mam.

Monty
She's nice.

Mam
Yes.

Monty
Take after her dad, does she?

Cynth (*staggers back in*)
Hot. Hot. Hot. Hot.

Monty
Hot?

Cynth nods and sits. Mam has been caught out. She disguises herself in some fashion.

Cynth
You his wife, then?

Mam shakes her head vigorously.

Monty
She's my fiancée.

Cynth
What's that?

Monty
She'll one day be my wife.

Cynth
Nice. Can I come to the wedding?

Mam shakes head.

Monty
Of course you can.

Cynth
Thanks. I've never been to a wedding. How's the soup?

Monty
Coming along. (*He tastes it.*) I'd say it really needs an onion to bring out the delicate flavour of the stone.

Cynth
I've got one of those!

Monty
Really?

Cynth

Yes.

She hands it over.

That was lucky.

Monty

Stay for some soup. It's delicious.
I've been a great traveller in my time.
I was just telling my fiancée here,
Mrs Banks-to-Be.
When I was a young one
(No older than you are now)
I thought I'd see the world.
So I did.
I got back to where I started
And stopped.
I couldn't make my mind up which way to go next.

The stones said to me
Why go anywhere? And shrugged
A million-year shrug.

The fire said to me
Warm who you touch, light the sky
And never ask why.

The water replied
Everything flows to the sea.
All becoming one.

And the air whispered
Here today, there tomorrow.
Breathe in, breathe out. Ssssh.

Asking where to go
I couldn't make up my mind.
I found I took root.

Now I'm travelling down
Through the earth's crust to its core.
Where will I get to?

So down through the past
I'm travelling now. New question –
Will my feet stick out?

You go round the world.
I found my biggest journey
In my own back yard.

Soup's ready.

*Monty fishes out the stone and pours a bowl for
Cynth.*

Cynth (*takes it*)
Thank you.

*Mam leaps forward, grabs it, tastes it. Adds salt.
Tastes it again. Adds pepper. Gives it to Cynth, who
doesn't think this is particularly unusual. Cynth takes
it and is about to eat when Mam takes it back, blows
on it. Tastes it again. Approves. Returns it to Cynth.*

Thanks, Mrs Banks-to-Be.

They all try the soup. Delish.

Thanks.
Where do you get those stones?
My mam would like one of them.

Monty
They're very special. They're stars that drop out of
the sky.

Cynth
I saw one! I saw one!
I did. I saw one.

It fell out of the sky.
I saw it.
Monty.
Now I know where I'm going.
And why.
I'll go and get it for my mam.
Now.
Can't stop to chat.

She falls asleep.

Right, I'm off.

Monty
Cynth.

Cynth
Yes, Monty?

Monty
Why don't you take this soup stone home to your mam.
I'm sure she'd like it.

Cynth
Thank you, Monty. Thank you very much.

She takes it. And throws all the things out of her bag.
Thinks better of it and keeps the home stone. And
then the soup stone. Mam is very pleased at this
development. Cynth sets off.

Monty
Erm, Cynth.

Cynth
Yes, Monty?

Monty
Home's not that way.

Cynth
I know.

Monty

Home's that way.

Cynth

I know.

But I'm not going home.

Monty

Oh?

Cynth

I'm looking for a star for my mam to make soup with.

Monty

But you've got one.

I gave you one.

Cynth

I know.

I'll keep it so I know what to look for when I find mine.

Then I'll bring yours back.

Mam, alarmed by the turn of events, stuffs everything back in her bag.

Got to go now. Goodbye.

Monty

Good luck.

Cynth

It's been very nice meeting you.

I hope you'll be very happy together.

Monty puts his arm round Mam.

I'm sure we will.

Cynth leaves.

Monty

I tried.

Mam
Thanks.

Monty (*his arm is still around her. Mmmm*)
Perhaps you should stay for a while.

Mam
In your back yard?

Monty
Yes. She needs to find out what's what.

Mam
She does.

Monty
And you look as if you know what's what already.

Mam
I do.

Monty
Let her go.

Mam (*springs apart*)
On her own?
Are you mad?
It's a scary world out there.
I've got to go.
Got to go.

Monty
You could come back.

Mam
I could come back here
On my way to somewhere else
But don't hold your breath.

Twilight. Autumn. Rain.

Cynth
 Wet. Wet. Wet. Wet.
 Rain. Rain. Rain. Rain.
 River. River? River!
 Stop.
 A river blocks my way,
 Deep, dark fast-flowing water.
 Fear sweeps me away.
 Look for a star.

She begins to search the bank.

Flint (*appears on the far bank*)
 Oi!
 Oi!
 Oi!

Cynth (*looks around*)
 Me?

Flint
 No, I'm talking to myself.
 I always do it very loud
 So that I pay attention.

Cynth
 Oh.
 I hope you're not telling yourself a secret because
   I can hear it too.
 You'd be better whispering.

Flint (*now to Cynth*) Oi.

Cynth ignores him.

 Oi!
 Oi!
 Oi!

Cynth
Me?

Flint
Yes.

Cynth
How am I supposed to know the difference?

Flint
I don't know.
What are you doing?

Cynth
Looking for a star.

Flint
In the mud?

Cynth
Yes.

Flint
You're looking in the wrong place.

Cynth
Where should I be looking?

Flint points up.

Cynth
I can't see any stars.

Flint
That's because it's raining.

Cynth
I know it's raining.
It's dribbling down my neck.
Thanks for telling me.

They look at each other. There is a strong attraction.

Cynth
What's your name?

Flint
Flint.

Cynth
That's a nice name.

Flint
What's your name?

Cynth
Cynth.

Flint
Hiya. That's a lovely name.
Lovely.

Cynth
My mam chose it.

Flint
It's lovely.
You're lovely.

Cynth
Me?

Flint
Yes.

Cynth
Thanks. So are you.
You're lovely too.

Flint
Thanks. Why are you looking for a star in the mud?

Cynth
For my mam.

Flint
Stars live in the sky.

Cynth
Some of them fall out.
I've seen one with my own eyes.
You don't know nothing.

Flint
I know where stars live.

Cynth
Do you know what's what?

Flint
What?

Cynth
I didn't think you did.

Flint
Where are you going?

Cynth
Somewhere else.

*I would like this to develop into a love dance –
together, but neither able to reach the other. It starts
lyrically but becomes more vigorous.*

Flint
Oi! Oi!
Come across.
Come over the river.

Cynth
Alright.
I can't.
It's too wide and too deep.

Flint
Use the stones.

Cynth
What?

Flint
Use the stones by the river.
Get one.

Cynth
Me?

Flint
Well, I can't.
I'm over here.

Cynth
Yes.

She hesitates.

Flint
Do you want to come?

Cynth
Yes.

Flint
Well then, get a stone.

Cynth does.

Put it in the water.

Cynth does.

Flint
Get another.

Cynth does.

Flint
Stand on the first.

Cynth does.

Flint
Put the stone down.

Cynth
Where?

Flint
In the water. But nearer me.

Cynth does.

Flint
Now stand on it.

Cynth does.

Flint
Pick up the first.

Cynth does.
Around this time Mam arrives and secretly watches.

Flint
Put it in the water.

Cynth does.

Flint
Stand on it.

Cynth does.

Flint
Now pick up the other.

Cynth does. Then stops.

Cynth
Flint.

Flint
What?

Cynth
You can stop telling me now.
I've got the idea.

Flint
Oh.
Sorry, Cynth.

Cynth
That's alright.

Cynth proceeds a few more. She's now in the middle.

Flint
What's wrong, Cynth?

Cynth
It's deep.

Flint
Keep coming.

Cynth
Flint.
I can't.

Flint
Why not?

Cynth
A river. Stepping stones.
Deep, dark fast-flowing water.
Fear sweeps me away.
I'm scared.

Flint
Throw me your bag.

Cynth does.

Flint
Is that better?

Cynth nods. She picks up a stone. She looks at Flint.

Flint
What?

Cynth
I can't come.
I'm scared.

Flint
Is there anything in here?

*He throws everything out of the bag. Tries to make
a rope from clothes.*

Cynth
Flint.

Flint
What?

Cynth
Can you hurry up.
Water's getting deeper.

The clothes rope is obviously too short.

Flint
I'll get help.
Wait there.

Cynth
Alright.
No choice.

Flint
Don't move.

Cynth

    Can't anyway.

He runs off.

Cynth sings loud.

Wet, wet, wet, wet.
River, river, river.
Stuck.
Deep deep deep.
Deeper deeper deeper.
Stuck.

She waits. He does not come.
    Mam appears in disguise again. She waves.

Cynth (*waves back*)

    Hello, Mrs Banks-to-Be.
    I'm waiting
    For Flint.
    He's gone for help.
    I'm stuck.
    Help.
    I need help.

Mam wades in. If she's brought the washing line with her she can maybe tie this to something.

It's deep. Very deep.
Getting darker every minute.
We're in big trouble.

Mam is washed away.

Can you swim, Mrs Banks-to-Be?
I can't.

Mam tries again and is washed away again.

My mam never taught me.
It's only a stream where we live.
I don't think she can swim.

Mam tries again and gets to her stone.
    Cynth gets in the water. Mam prepares to bring
them back.

No.
Not that way
I've got to keep going.
Mam needs her star
And Flint will come back.

This is a mammoth struggle. Mam supports Cynth,
who still has her stone, and finally Cynth nearly
drowns Mam as she gets onto the shore.
    They snuggle. Cold, wet and shivery.

Better wait here for Flint.
He'll be back soon.
Would you like some soup to warm you up,
    Mrs Banks-to-Be?

She puts a stone in a tin.

There. That shouldn't take long,

She falls asleep.
    Mam quickly supplies vegetables, seasoning and
fire. She sits and waits.

Mam
Flint will not come back.
Like your dad with me and you.
No they never do.
Oh Cynth.

Cynth (*wakes up*)
Waking up to rain.

Stone sky, stone face, heart of rock
Heavy in my chest.
Is the soup ready?

Mam nods.

Cynth
It works.
I can do it.

*Gives some soup to Mam, who gets some salt out to
flavour it, thinks better of it, puts it away and tucks in.*

Wet wet wet wet.
Mam must be washing.
Good drying day blows the rain away somewhere else.
This must be somewhere else.

You're a good swimmer.
Mam can't do that.
Mam can't do nothing much.

Still raining.
No Flint.

He's not coming, is he?

Mam shakes head.

He doesn't love me, does he?
He took my things.
Except my stones.

I'm going to find a star for Mam
On my own.
Then she can make soup too.

Goodbye, Mrs Banks-to-Be,
It has been very nice talking to you.

*She leaves. Mam sits. Flint arrives, in a flap, with
a rope.*

Flint

Cynth. Cynth, I'm back.

He sees she's gone. He looks at the water.

Oh no.
Not in the water. Cynth. Cynth.
Help me. Somebody help me.

Sees Mam.

Have you seen a girl? Here.

Mam

Yes.

Flint

Where is she?
Not in the river.

Mam

Not any more. I fished her out.

Flint

Is she alright?

Mam

No thanks to you.

Flint

Thank goodness.
I love her.

Mam

What?

Flint

I love her.

Mam (*assaults him*)

Then why did you leave her then?
You love her so much, why did you run off?

Eh?
Eh?

Flint
For help. (*He holds up a rope.*)

Mam (*she's continuing to take it out on him*)
Why didn't you swim to her?

Flint
I can't swim.
I can't.

Mam
Well you should learn.
What are your parents thinking of, sending you out
into the world?
Not swim?!
You might drown.

Flint
Have you finished?

Mam
Yes.

Flint
Cynth can't swim either.

Mam
I know, I'm her mother.

Flint
Oh. Pleased to meet you.

Mam doesn't reply.

Flint
Don't you think you should have . . .?

Mam
What?

Flint

    Nothing.

Mam

    I can't think of everything.

Flint

    Where is she?

Mam

    She's gone.

Flint

    Which way? I've got to find her.

    Mam points in the opposite direction to the way
    Cynth in fact went.

Flint

    Thank you.

Mam

    Don't mention it.

Night. Winter. Snow.
    By the ocean. Cynth is very tired. Trudging along.
Mam is accompanying her. Cynth is only barely aware
of her. This is a dance, Mam quietly supporting Cynth
along the way. Mam is stepping in Cynth's footsteps.
    How silent is snow.
    Even thought is too loud here.
    Soft white silence falls.

Cynth

    Cold, cold, cold, cold.

    Where have I come to?

    Footprints show where I've come from.

Where am I going?
Ocean.
Where to now?
Must be somewhere.
Looks like nowhere.
Make soup.
Stone in pan.
Snow will melt.

Puts stone in pan.
Goes to sleep.

Mam looks in her bag for ingredients. Can't find
any. Is frantic. Looks around. Nothing. Races off
backwards, placing her feet in the footprints.
    Cynth wakes up.

Soup.

A man comes along the beach.

Cynth
Hello, I'm Cynth.

Man starts to rifle through her stuff.

What are you doing?

Man
What have you got?

Cynth
What have I got?

Man
Hat.

Cynth
Hat?

Man
Hat.
Gizzit.

Cynth does.

Man
Coat.

Cynth
Coat?

Man
Coat.
Gizzit.

Cynth does.

Man
Shoes.

Cynth
Shoes?

Man
Shoes.
Gizzem.

Cynth does.

Man
Anything else?

Cynth
Anything else?

Man
Anything else.

Cynth (*looks at the stone soup*)
No.

Man
What's that?

Cynth
No.

Man
  Show me.

Cynth
  No. No.

  A battle ensues. Cynth hangs on to the pot like grim death but finally he wrenches it from her.

Man (*empties it*)
  Stones? It's just stones? Why did you fight so hard
    for stones?

  He throws them on the ground, and goes.

Cynth (*shocked by this, gathers her stones*)
  Stones?
  Not just stones.
  That's my home stone
  That's my stepping stone
  And that's my star stone.
  And it makes soup.

  Puts stone in pan.

  Stone.
  Must need longer.

  She puts it back in. She walks up and down, trying to get warm.

  Cold. Cold. Cold. Cold.
  Here I am
  On my own.
  Middle of the night.
  Where am I?
  On my own.
  All this way
  Without Mam.
  Soup.

Pours out of the pan again, a stone.

Stone.

She tastes it.

It's cold and tasteless.
Stone.
Cold stone.
Stone cold.

Mam comes racing in, hands full of veg. Sees her.
Stops.

Wish I'd never come.
Sitting on the cold hard rock.
Wish I'd stayed at home
With my mam.
Oh Mam.
I need you now.
Mam!

Mam is torn. Silently echoes her pain. It's agony, but
she doesn't reveal herself.

Cynth (*looks up. Looks around. Sees Mam*)
Mrs Banks-to-Be! What are you doing here?
Are you alright?
You don't look alright.
I know what you need.
You need some soup!

She gives her the pan. Mam tastes it.

Not very nice, is it?
It just needs a few carrots to bring out the flavour.

Mam gives her some and Cynth starts to make the
soup.

A potato would be nice.
Is that an onion?
Let's wait for it to cook.
These are my stones.
This one is from my home.
Where's your home, Mrs Banks-to-Be?

*All of this should be indicated in a way other than
speech while Cynth interprets. In the first production,
Mam used British Sign Language.*

Far away?
Me too.
Is that where you come from?

Mam
No.

Cynth
Where are you from?

Mam
Here. This place.

Cynth
Here?
By the sea?

Mam
This is where I grew up.
Fishing.
Swimming.

Cynth
Why did you leave?

Mam digs under the snow and finds a charred stone.

It's burned.
Did something bad happen here?

Mam

Yes. A war.
A lot of fighting.
People were killed.

Cynth

What about your family?

Mam

All killed.
My parents. My brothers and sister.
Our house burned down.

Cynth

What happened to you?

Mam

I hid and managed to escape.
I fell in love with a soldier.

Cynth

What happened?

Mam

I thought we'd be together for ever.

Cynth

Were you?

Mam

No.
When he found out I was expecting a baby he didn't
want to know.

Cynth

What did you do?

Mam

I left.
I went far, far away from here.
As far away as I could get.

Cynth

What about the baby?

Mam

It was a little girl.

Cynth

And I expect you looked after her and loved her,
    didn't you?

Mam

Yes.

Cynth

What happened to her?

Mam

She's grown up now.
She has her own life.
She knows what's what.

Cynth

But she still needs her mam though, doesn't she?

Mam

I don't think so.

Cynth

I still need mine.
I'm going back to see her now.
This stone is from my home so I can find my way back.
This one is a stepping stone.
I'll take one from here to show her how far I came.
And I want to take her a soup stone.
But I don't think I'll find one here
Not unless it drops out of the sky on my head.

*Both Mam and Cynth look up expectantly. There is
a shifting under the snow and stones. Something is
emerging. Cynth jumps back. Mam stands frozen as*

*a pair of feet burst up like a tree. They are holding
a stone.*

Cynth

Monty!
Monty, you made it!
It's me, Cynth.
And you'll never guess who's here too.
Mrs Banks-to-Be!
Say hello to Monty, Mrs Banks-to-Be.

*Mam says 'Hi' to the feet in some way. Maybe has a
pair of socks to put on them.*

And Monty.
You found me a soup stone.
Thanks.
I'm taking it home for my mam now.
Goodbye, Mrs Banks-to-Be.
It's been very nice listening to you.

*Now I would like this to be a mad celebratory dash
back though the environments of the play.*

Up the stony snowy beach.

Cold cold cold cold.

Across the river.

Wet wet wet wet.

Past Monty.

Hot hot hot hot.

Cynth returns his soup stone.

Thanks, Monty.

Mam gives him a kiss.

Mam
Thanks, Monty.
How's your back yard?

Monty
Getting a bit boring.

Mam
Maybe you'd like to come and have a look at mine?

Monty
Maybe I would.
By the way –

Mam
What?

Monty
What's your name?

Mam
Bonny.
See you.

*Back to the windy home with Mam making it back
narrowly before Cynth.*

Cynth
Home home home home.

Mam
Sun on the mountain.
Sunshine comes up. Come up sun.
Sunshine come up sun.

Cynth
Mam. Mam. Mam.
I'm home, Mam.

Mam
Hello, Cynth.
Welcome home.

Cynth

> Home. Where I began
> And after long travelling
> Where I ended. Home.

Mam

> You must be hungry.
> I'll get you something to eat.

Cynth

> No.
> Stay put.
> I've brought you a present.
> Here.
> It's a soup stone,

Mam

> Thank you.

Cynth

> I'll tell you how to use it.
> You need veg to bring out the flavour.
> I didn't find out what's what.
> You'll have to tell me.

Mam

> Me?

Cynth

> Yes.
> You do answers.

Mam

> Oh.

> *Thinks.*

> No.
> I knew what's what once.

I used to do answers.
Now I'm all questions again.

While the soup is being made, Flint turns up.

Flint
Oi!
Hello, Cynth.

Cynth
Hiya. What are you doing here?

Flint
Come to see you.
A lady told me which way
But I got lost.

Cynth
Mam. This is Flint.

Mam
Hello.

Flint
Hiya.

Mam
Does he know what's what?

Cynth
No.
But he's nice.
Can he stay for soup?

Mam
You're cooking it. He can stay if you like.

Cynth
Yes. I do like.
You can stay.

Flint
Thanks.

They sit.

Cynth
This soup is made from a star
By me.

They eat.

Cynth (*notices something*)
Mam! Mam! Mam!
What's that?

Mam
What?

Cynth
That. That. That.
That apple tree there.
That wasn't there when I went.

Mam
It grew from the apple you dropped.

Cynth
Eating an apple
I dropped it and ran away.
Return to a tree!

Mam
You planted a tree.
Walked away, no looking back.
It grew. So did you.

The stars in the sky.
They seem to have always been.
Suddenly one moves
And everything must change.

End.

JUMPING ON MY SHADOW

Peter Rumney

*a play for eight- to twelve-year-olds
and their families*

My thanks to those refugees and asylum seekers
who have agreed to share their stories,
whether recent or from the distant past,
to the many children who have considered
some of the play's questions, and to all the adults
who have helped make and shape the play.

Jumping on My Shadow was first presented in May 2001 by Theatre Centre at the Half Moon Theatre, London, prior to a national tour. It was revived for a further tour from September to December 2001. The cast was as follows:

Mr Miah, Caretaker, Official 1 Antony Bunsee
Grandmother, Official 2 Karen Glossop
Anna, Official 3 Isobel Suttie
Josip Tumi Lambo

Director Rosamunde Hutt
Writer's Consultant Joyoti Grech
Dramaturge Noel Greig
Designer Anna Fleischle
Design Assistant Caroline Thaw
Composer Hettie Malcolmson
Company Stage Manager Samantha Nurse/Marijke Swart
Movement Director Chix Chandria
Lighting Designer Jane Mackintosh
Production Manager Claire Henders
Voice Consultant Bernadette O'Brien
Associate Artist William Elliott
Sign Language Interpreter Jacqui Beckford

Characters

From 2002

Josip

Mr Miah

Caretaker

Official 1

From 1959

Grandmother

Anna

Official 2

Official 3

Act One

PROLOGUE

*The audience are 'called' in song to the performance
space, in the original production by the sound of Josip
playing his mbira (thumb piano).*

They take their seats.

A steel-walled city.

A small bakery.

Steel walls enclosing, defining or blocking the space.

*An oven, a table, chairs, a walk-through, full-length
see-through mirror, the paraphernalia of making bread.*

Images of travel and migration.

*People are travelling from one place to another in
order to migrate, some under extreme pressure: a coach
of women leaving Srebrenica; a group of young men
disembarking from the* Windrush; *South Vietnamese
civilians trying to get into the American Embassy; a
group of East End evacuees is welcomed by rural foster-
parents; a line of cars at the Kosovan–Macedonian
border; Palestinians at the West Bank; West Africans
waiting at a Spanish enclave; an American businessman
in an airport hospitality lounge; Iraqis attempting to
enter Australia; trains of displaced people slowly
traversing the Indian subcontinent . . .*

*We see each 'story' for a few seconds, just long
enough to understand the emotional impact of the
journey/departure/arrival, without dwelling on it or
making a value judgement of any kind.*

*A tapestry of global movement to begin a new life,
temporary or permanent.*

*There may also be images of the mechanics of
transportation: aircraft taking off and landing, the view*

*through a porthole in a plane, from a ship, a ship
docking, a bullock cart, Eurostar, cattle trucks . . .*

*Grandmother is slowly and rhythmically kneading
bread dough.*

*She is thinking about something, absorbed in her
work. She does not relate to the surroundings beyond
her immediate workplace.*

Mr Miah waits. He wears a campaign medal.

Josip exits.

Mr Miah A small bakery
In a city, on a river near the sea
A small bakery (No 15 left-hand side).
A city . . .
A gateway to the east . . .

A wall.
The Emperor's wall.
Keeping people out.
Out of the city.

Outside the wall, the wind, *seven* winds, blowing from
seven corners of the world, gust upon gust of chill wind
blows desperate people towards the safety of this city,
blows them to the wall, knocking on the Emperor's wall,
banging at the Eastern gate, 'Let us in, let us in to the
city, let us in to the City of Bread' . . .

Knocking.

The sound of an aircraft landing overhead.

Mr Miah becomes the Caretaker.

*His uniform is ubiquitous. He wears a peaked cap.
He could be from anywhere, at any time in recent
history.*

Grandmother continues making bread, oblivious.

SCENE ONE: ANYTIME

An indecipherable female voice calmly gives airport announcements in a non-specific language. We could be anywhere.
  The Caretaker patrols the space and the wall.

Caretaker (*to audience*) Knock-knock! . . . Who's there? . . . Boo!!! . . . Boo who? . . . Aah, no need to cry! Hahaha!
  Knock-knock . . . Who's there? . . . Police . . . Police who? . . . Police let me in, it's freezing out here! Ha ha ha! . . .
  Knock-knock . . . Who's there? . . .

Quiet knocking from behind the wall.

Just a minute.

The Caretaker feels the wall, examines it, checking for sound, cracks, tarnishing.

I don't like the look of this.

Grandmother is pummelling the dough.
  There is a louder banging from the other side of the wall. Harsh voices. The banging increases in intensity. The Caretaker backs off in alarm.
  Grandmother is kneading the dough gently.

(*to himself*) I knew it, I knew it! (*to the audience*) They're trying to get in! (*calling off*) Inform the Emperor immediately!

The banging on the wall continues.
  Grandmother is carefully removing her apron and clearing up any of her own mess.

(*to the audience*) Enough's enough, a limit's a limit . . .

Grandmother makes an unhurried exit.

(*towards the wall*) Filthy, dirty, rubbish, go away!

The banging continues, becoming more urgent.

Curses, curses!! (*Shouts.*) Call Security! Call Pest Control! Call the Emperor's Guard!!

The knocking continues.
A hand appears through the wall.
The Caretaker backs away.

You can't come in, whoever you are, we don't want you here!

A repeat of the aircraft / airport announcement sounds, as . . .
A foot, then a leg appears through the wall.

Help! Help! This is an emergency! . . .

Josip emerges through the gap in the wall with difficulty. He breathes heavily. They stare at each other in mutual terror for a moment.

Help! Help! Call the Emperor's Guard!!

The Caretaker exits.

SCENE TWO: NOW

Josip stands in the performance space. A boy with nothing: escapee, refugee, asylum seeker.
We hear a snatch of a harsh refrain, male voice(s) speaking in an unknown language from Josip's past. It sounds as if peremptory orders are being given. Josip stiffens.
A snatch of music from Josip's homeland filters into the space as if emerging from his memory . . . powerful, painful, lament . . .

He closes his eyes, allows the music into himself. It carries him away from this space back to his abandoned home.

Josip I am . . . boy from nowhere . . . I am boy from nowhere . . .

A repetition of the harsh voices cuts in, followed by a repetition of the aircraft noises and airport announcements.
    Josip is 'present' in the space once again.

I am boy from nowhere . . .

Grandmother I hate this day . . .
    I hate this day . . .
    I hate this day . . .

Music.

SCENE THREE: THEN

The focus of the performance space changes as actors' movements and directions make new patterns in space.
    Josip is left trying to find his bearings.
    Grandmother sings a niggun (*wordless prayer*) *from 'the Old Country'. She goes to the mirror and looks at herself.*
    Josip exits.

Mr Miah A bakery,
    An old old bakery,
    No 15, on the left-hand side of the street,
    Now
    And then . . .

Grandmother is brushing her hair in the mirror.

The future, past, we mix them up like so much flour and water, to make, to bake the story.

Grandmother is getting a chair and reaching up to a small, black and white photograph, hidden perhaps somewhere in the steel wall.

A tale of ghosts, of secrets, of memories . . . and of bread!

Mr Miah exits.
  Grandmother is sitting on the chair and looking at the photo.
  She opens the hot oven and puts the photograph inside to destroy it. She waits for a moment. She cannot go through with it. She removes the scalded photo, blows on it and then moves the chair in order to put the photo back in its hiding place.
  Anna, her granddaughter, has entered and stands watching her, unnoticed.
  Grandmother is reaching up to hide the photograph.

Anna I'm back, Grandma . . .

Grandmother Oh!!! You made me jump!

Anna Sorry.

Grandmother It's alright, darling, only . . .

Anna Sorry . . .

Grandmother . . . don't sneak up on people, particularly at my age, oohf . . .

Anna Sorry, I didn't mean to . . .

Grandmother It's alright, darling, I know . . .

Anna Are you alright?

Grandmother I know . . . yes, no, I'm alright . . .

Anna What were you doing with the chair?

Grandmother Nothing! With the chair? . . . Nothing.

She goes to kiss Anna. Anna avoids it. Grandmother is taken aback.

You alright?

Anna Yes yes . . .

Grandmother What's the matter?

Anna Nothing . . .

Grandmother studies Anna for a moment, then puts the brush down and gathers the ingredients to make bread.
Throughout the following scene the characters are engaged in making and kneading eggy yeast dough. The suggested details can change but must counterpoint and drive the character's action along.

Grandmother Good, well . . . come on, the table needs a wipe.

Anna Must I?

Grandmother Yes.

Anna (*unenthusiastic*) What are we making?

Grandmother Bread, what do you think?

Anna Story bread?

Grandmother Of course . . .

Anna . . . Story bread, great . . . (*She grabs something as if to start.*)

Grandmother (*grabbing the object off her*) Just a minute, just for once be patient!

Anna (*shrugs*) Sorry. Why is it called story bread again?

Grandmother (*testing the temperature of the water, then adding it to the bowl*) This you should know . . .

Anna Of course I know, I just want you to tell me . . .

Grandmother (*opening bag of flour*) Because when you break the loaf open, all the stories from the Old Country escape for a breather . . .

Anna What do you mean, 'Old Country', exactly?

Grandmother (*darker*) The Old Country.

Anna Do you mean where you came from?

Grandmother (*shifting tack*) When you break open the loaf all the old stories come out for a bit of a nose around, that's why the bread smells so good . . .

Anna Yes, I know, but how come there are stories inside the bread?

Grandmother How come?

Anna Yes, how come the stories get inside in the first place?

Grandmother (*weighing the flour*) How come, how come . . . every day we bake fresh bread to eat, no? Of course, it's natural, the bread goes back since, I don't know, since way-before-when, it reminds us of our history . . . The bread reminds us of who we *were* – (*tapping the scales*) – and who we *are* . . . Pass the large bowl, no that one, thank you, so, without the bread your *body*'s starving, . . .

Anna (*joining in at the same time*) . . . *body*'s starving . . .

Grandmother (*puts flour in the bowls*) . . . and without the stories your *soul*'s starving . . .

Anna (*at the same time*) . . . your *soul*'s starving! . . .

Grandmother . . . so, when we make story bread we're killing two birds with one stone. (*Adds the salt.*) It's very economical, if you think about it. Now, Anna, sift the flour and the salt together – *carefully*, please, I don't want flour everywhere . . .

> *They begin sifting, Grandmother efficiently, Anna more dreamily.*
> *A snatch of music, faint (Mr Miah's theme perhaps).*
> *Grandmother stops, goes to the oven, opens it, sniffs, closes it again.*

Anna What is it?

Grandmother Nothing. Wonderful smell . . . Nothing . . .

> *They continue with the mixing.*

Anna Grandma Eva . . .

Grandmother Yes, child?

Anna *Please* don't call me 'child', Grandma.

Grandmother Yes, Anna, darling? (*Adds water and yeast.*)

Anna Don't call me '*darling*', I'm not your boyfriend, you know . . .

Grandmother Yes, *Anna*?

Anna How long have you been in this country?

Grandmother A long time.

Anna How long?

Grandmother Long enough . . . Pass me the butter while it's still runny, please . . .

239

Anna (*she does so*) How old were you when you came here?

Grandmother (*putting the butter in large bowls*) Not much older than you, three, four years older maybe, I forget . . .

Anna Really?

Grandmother (*mixing the batter*) Yes really. Now move, please, Anna, you're not wearing an apron, I told you always to wear the apron . . .

Anna But you're not wearing one . . .

Grandmother That's not the point.

Anna Grandma, that's completely the point, you . . .

Grandmother Enough with the cheek.

Anna What cheek? I'm just saying . . .

Grandmother And *I'm* just saying, your *own* laundry you do it if you get egg on your dress . . .

Anna I *won't* get egg on my dress, I'm not a *baby* you know . . .

Grandmother Put the apron on, *now* . . .

Anna Yes, yes . . .

Grandmother And less of the 'yes, yes'.

Anna Yes, yes, Grandma . . . (*Anna puts the apron on without doing up the strings.*)

Grandmother And do it properly!

> They knead the dough together without talking.
> A snatch of Mr Miah's or Josip's theme.
> Grandmother suddenly stops again.

Where's it coming from?

Anna What?

Grandmother Nothing. I can smell something, can't put my finger on it . . .

Anna Of course you can't put your finger on it, it's a smell, you can't put your finger on a smell, there's nothing there!

Grandmother It's as if somebody else is cooking here as well . . . (*Looks at Anna a moment.*) Anyway, it's nothing, just my age, I'm losing my marbles . . .

Anna You need a nice, strong cup of tea, Grandma, I'll make you one.

Grandmother It's just my imagination. Er, no thank you, Anna, later maybe.

They continue kneading the dough.

Anna Grandma, have you ever seen the Emperor?

Grandmother No.

Anna Has anyone ever seen the Emperor?

Grandmother Shouldn't think so.

Anna Did you have an emperor where you came from?

Grandmother No.

Anna Have you always lived at No 15?

Grandmother Enough questions, I can't concentrate . . . .

Anna Grandma, did you come here with your parents?

Grandmother Stop it, Anna . . .

Anna Did you have to come here on your own?

Grandmother Stop it . . .

Anna Didn't you have any brothers or sisters?

Grandmother Stop it, stop it . . .

Grandmother grabs Anna's arm and looks at her intently.

Stop it, stop it! I don't want to talk about it, some things you talk about, some things you don't . . .

Anna You're hurting my arm . . .

Grandmother Do you understand? . . . Anna! . . .

Anna Grandma, you're hurting my arm! . . .

Pause.

Grandmother I'm sorry, I'm sorry. (*She attacks the dough.*) Have some honey, yes?

Anna (*partly mollified*) Yes please.

Grandmother (*puts the honey in Anna's mouth, then has some herself*) I shouldn't really. Never mind . . .

Anna That *really* hurt, you know . . .

Grandmother It's probably just your growing pains, Anna.

Anna It's not 'growing pains', you hurt my arm . . .

Grandmother I said I was sorry.

Anna . . . *and* you got dough on my dress.

Grandmother It was a *mistake* . . .

Anna No, but . . .

Grandmother Enough with the guilt, I said I was sorry, I didn't mean to hurt you . . .

Anna But you did . . .

Grandmother I didn't *mean* to . . .

Anna No but Grandma . . .

Grandmother No buts, no bathwater. Enough.

Anna struggles with this phrase for a moment. They continue with the kneading, both attacking the dough. Then:

Anna *Why* don't you want to talk about it?

Grandmother Anna!

Anna No, no, listen, Grandma, pretend – *pretend* you don't know me. I'm a stranger, I've just walked in through the door like, just like, 'Hello,' no notice, no invitation, no family, out of the blue . . .

Throwing the dough in the air and generally turning the next section into a bit of a performance.

. . . and you decide I'm your *long-lost imaginary grand-daughter*, because I'm so *lovely* . . .

Grandmother Stop that, you'll drop it . . .

Anna So here I am, one dress and a pair of socks to stand up in, otherwise nothing, apart from a funny accent, just, 'Yes-no-thank-you-please,' so you decide to adopt me, 'cos you're *quite nice really*, to adopt me as your *lovely granddaughter* . . .

Grandmother (*laughing*) Enough! Pass me the flour and . . . don't . . .

Anna (*dropping something*) Sorry, sorry it was an accident.

Grandmother (*knocking something over herself and losing control*) It's always the same, Anna . . . (*to herself*) I hate this day, I hate the twenty-seventh.

Anna What's the date got to do with it?

Grandmother Right, finish the dough, and put it in to rise . . . Put it in the warm . . .

Anna (*still kneading*) Where are you going?

Grandmother (*containing herself*) I'm going to get some poppy seeds, I've run out of poppy seeds . . .

Anna No you haven't, there's some in the . . .

Grandmother I have to go *out*, alright? Don't turn the oven up until I get back, or we'll all go up in smoke.

A momentary shadow passes over Grandmother, then she wants to get out.

Remember to lock the door after me, and don't forget the mess . . .

Grandmother is exiting.

Anna Yes, yes, Grandma, bye . . . .

Grandmother I won't be long . . .

Grandmother exits.

Anna What did your *last* slave die of?

Anna puts the dough in a bowl, covering it with a dishcloth and putting it in an appropriate place to rise. She sees the hairbrush forgotten, out of place.

Ahah! 'Hopeless grandparent who never remembers to put anything away,' blah, blah, blah . . . Ugh, yuck . . . grey hairs, disgusting . . .

Anna cleans the brush, goes to the mirror, and slowly starts to brush her own hair.
She gazes at herself in the mirror.

Hello, Anna . . .

She sings a brief snatch of her Grandmother's song.

(*exaggerated sweet smile*) 'Helloo.' (*angry at adult face*) 'Anna do this, Anna do that . . .' (*disdain*) What did your *last* slave die of?' (*straightforward, gazing, to herself*) Hello, Anna . . . (*Then she remembers the photograph. Exclaims.*) Photograph! (*She grabs the same chair and reaches up for the photograph.*) Nearly, come on, you can reach . . . yes!

> *A very old photograph of Grandmother and a*
> *younger sister.*
> > *Anna sits on the chair.*
> > *Sound of train getting steam up, a platform whistle.*

Two girls . . . a railway station? Two girls with plaited hair . . . It's you . . . it's you, Grandma. Who's the other one holding your hand, and a lady not smiling? Grandma? . . .

> *A repeat of aircraft sound and airport announcements.*
> > *Mr Miah enters. He is singing a song. An equivalent to Grandmother's original niggun. He is doing something with 'Grandmother's' flour, utensils, etc.*
> > *Anna returns the photograph to its original position.*
> > *Mr Miah and Anna move round each other again. It's clear they are in the same space, but at a different time and unaware of each other.*
> > *Mr Miah exits.*

SCENE FOUR: NOW

A repeat of the aircraft and airport announcements.
> *Josip repeats his earlier entry through the wall.*
> *Anna takes off apron, puts it on chair and exits.*

Josip (*exactly repeating previous statement to himself*) I am boy from nowhere . . .

Officials 2 and 3 arrive. It is the last interview of the day.

Official 2 Let's try again, shall we, er – (*Looks at document.*) Josip? (*Pronounces name incorrectly.*)

Josip (*shakes his head*) Yes . . .

Official 2 (*shakes slowly*) No, no, your name is . . . Josip, yes?

Josip (*shakes*) Yes, yes!

Official 2 (*shakes*) No!

Josip (*nods*) N-no?

Official 2 (*shakes*) No!

Josip (*nods faster*) No, no!

Official 2 is exasperated

Official 3 Perhaps I can help here . . . Where you come from, Josip – (*Correct pronunciation.*) – it is the custom to shake your head when you say 'Yes,' and to nod your head when you say 'No,' yes?

Josip (*shakes*) Yes, yes!

Official 3 But unfortunately, here, we *nod* – (*Does it.*) – to say 'Yes,' and *shake* – (*Does it.*) – to say 'No,' yes? (*Smiles.*) You understand?

Josip (*shakes his head*) Yes . . . (*Nods his head.*) Ah, no . . . ah . . .

Official 2 (*losing patience*) This is not helping us, we need to know *why* you've come here, *how* you've managed to get in, why you have come on your *own*, and of course to ensure that you are looked after properly until you're . . . until your case is decided. We'll need a Form B23.

Josip (*nods tentatively*) Yes . . .

Official 3 (*filling out form*) I'll arrange for someone to look after you, and in the morning we'll have another go, alright?

Josip (*shakes, then corrects himself and nods*) Yes!

Official 2 And remember . . . under the Emperor's new rules, most people we send back.

> *Music* (*the music Josip heard at his first arrival*).
> *The Officials take Josip's fingerprints.*
> *The Officials exeunt.*
> *The sound of the outside street.*
> *Mr Miah enters with a bowl of water for Josip to wash his hands.*
> *Josip gives him Form B23, then washes his hands.*
> *He offers Josip a jacket, a toothbrush, a blanket.*
> *The sound fades.*

Mr Miah Welcome to my home, Josip. My name is Mr Miah. It is my job to look after you.

> *Mr Miah gives Josip an old envelope with an address written on the back.*

Here is our address in case you get lost, No 15, but everybody knows where to find me. Just ask for the Bakery. *Tomar buk lakseni*, are you hungry?

Josip (*shakes his head carefully*) No . . . thank you.

Mr Miah You're tired. We'll talk in the morning. Sleep well. Welcome to the City of Bread.

> *Mr Miah exits.*

SCENE FIVE: NOW

Josip is alone, isolated in the space
  He produces his mbira and plays quietly for a moment.

Josip I am boy from nowhere
  I am small thought
  in big place,
  in hidden corner of big city
  that is never still,
  never quiet.

  Mbira very briefly again.

  The bakery never sleeps.
  In the smallest moment of night
  I hear damp yeast rising
  in the baker's cupboard,
  a promise for tomorrow.

  My thoughts rise,
  they swell,
  they feed on air around them,
  never still, never quiet,
  as I lie here alone, awake,
  a boy from nowhere in a small room.

  The sound of a wind in the distance. Josip shivers.

  A tiny sound is
  working its way around
  the narrow streets of the city
  like a clever wind coming this way . . .

  I can hear the wind-sound
  rubbing its back against the
  brick wall,
  tapping at the window,
  looking for me . . .

Sound of glass window breaking.

The glass cracks,
shatters all over the bed,
and the wind reaches in,
the wind grabs my thoughts and tosses them out into
    the night . . .

Everything hangs in the air for a moment,

Sound of wind in street.

then the wind tugs me up,
up above the narrow streets,
floating above the city like a thin angel.
I'm stretching my thin arms towards the east,
looking for dawn, sunlight,
looking for my father,
looking for my mother,
but as the sun rises in the east
a grey shadow rises also,
a grey shadow lifting its head and looking towards me
with cruel eyes as it moves towards me . . .

Distant sound of birds of prey circling.

Down below,
children are laughing in the street
jumping on my shadow as I reach towards them,
but they run away,
and I hear the cold laughter behind me,
and I feel the thin, bony hand that is flying towards
    me from the place I come from,
clutching at my clothes,
dirty fingernails scraping, scratching at my skin,
    pulling at my hair as I dive towards the broken
    window, fingernails scraping, scratching at my
    body . . . .

Sound.

Uh! (*Wakes.*)

The sound of the outside street.

Grey bird scratch on window.
It look at me with head on one side.
Outside is full of children's laugh,
and lorry moves slowly up street.
I smell bread.
Time for school.

Act Two

SCENE SIX: THEN AND NOW

As characters 'materialise' in the midst of each other's time frames there may be sound, steam, smoke, light, to suggest these apparitions.

On at least one occasion the characters will use the same utensil or implement in their work, but oblivious to each other.

Anna enters.

Josip goes to the mirror to practise his nods and shakes. They don't see each other, but cross each other's path.

Anna A scratching noise woke me up, a pigeon scratching on the window pane. I could hear laughter outside, and the sound of horses' hooves on the cobblestones. I smelled the bread. Late for school again!

Josip exits.

Anna checks to see that the photograph is there. She can now reach it easily.

A very brief résumé of her previous antics in the mirror, then she grabs an old school bag and exits, as Josip returns with a newer school bag and a baseball cap, and goes straight to the mirror.

(*on way out*) Late for school again!

Josip is looking in the mirror at a bruise on his head. It is tender.

Mr Miah comes in.

Josip immediately covers up the bruise with his cap and starts practising nods and shakes.

Mr Miah goes straight to the warm oven and removes Grandmother's dough. He is about to engage in the second stage of preparing spice bread after the dough has risen.

Mr Miah Good afternoon, Josip . . . *Tumi tik asoni*, how are we today?

Josip (*pause*) Okay.

Mr Miah Yes?

Josip I practise good, sir, they must understand me good.

Mr Miah How *was* school today, better?

Josip (*brief pause*) Okay.

Mr Miah (*stops what he's doing*) *Shob tik aseni*, you sure?

Josip Mmm, yes, okay . . .

Mr Miah Some of the boys still laughing at you?

Josip Mr Miah, I no go back . . .

Mr Miah Josip, I'm afraid you *must* go back . . .

Josip No! I no go . . .

Mr Miah Yes, yes, you *must* go back to school, every day, *kub dorhari*, it's *very* important, and I *insist* . . .

Josip No no, not school, not school, my country, my country . . .

Mr Miah (*as Josip speaks*) Ah . . .

Josip I no want go back my country . . . .

Mr Miah Yes . . .

Josip Is *very* bad I go home to my country . . .

Mr Miah Yes . . .

Josip Bad things, please . . .

Mr Miah I know . . .

Josip Please, Mr M . . . Mr, um . . .

Mr Miah Miah! . . .

Josip Mr M . . . Miah, Emperor's police, they send me back?

Mr Miah (*pause*) I don't know, Josip . . .

Josip When they say?

Mr Miah I don't *know*, Josip. I'm sorry, I just don't know.

Josip They send me *back*?

Mr Miah I don't *know*, Josip, maybe, we have to wait for the letter. I don't *know* . . .

Josip (*starts kicking the table etc.*) No! . . . No! . . .

Mr Miah Josip! . . .

Josip (*still kicking*) No!!

Mr Miah No, Josip, what do you think you're doing? Josip! . . .

> *Josip continues kicking.*
> *Grandmother enters, goes to the photograph, gets it down, looks at it briefly, puts it back, goes to a chair, sits, shuts her eyes.*

Stop that right now!

> *A couple more deliberate kicks in defiance.*
> *They face off to each other.*

Josip, I hope, I very much hope that you can stay. But we have to wait. We have to wait and see . . .

Pause. Mr Miah decides to attend to the baking.
   He puts on Anna's apron.

Hungry?

   Josip does not react.

Josip?

Josip Sorry, Mr Miah.

Mr Miah Yes. I am aware it has been bad for you. We just need some rules, yes?

Josip (*brief pause*) Okay.

Mr Miah Okay, good. Now, are you hungry?

Josip What you making?

Mr Miah *Aba*'s spice bread. Want to help me?

Josip (*still thinking about other things*) Okay.

Mr Miah *Bala, bala, kub bala.* ['*Good, very good.*']
I could do with a hand.

Josip You make much?

Mr Miah First we must wash, of course, I'll show you exactly how . . .

   Music.
      They wash hands in a ritual fashion. Then Mr Miah divides the dough in two and puts half on the table to work with, the rest back in Grandmother's bowl.

Josip You make much bread, Mr Miah?

   Mr Miah starts 'knocking back' the dough.

Mr Miah *Tik ase, tik ase*, definitely, my spice bread is famous in these parts. Just like *Aba* made.

Josip Who is *Aba*? . . .

Mr Miah *Aba* is 'father' in my language

Josip Oh, in my language 'father' is *Baba*! *Aba, Baba*!

Mr Miah Really? Extraordinary! Well I suppose we all had the same word once, back in the mists of time . . .

Josip (*laughing*) *Baba! Aba, Baba, Aba, Baba!*

Mr Miah Well, anyway . . . My father, *Allahi tandre behesh nosib horoka*, God watch over him, my father made the bread this way. Josip, if you would be so kind as to pass the spice, yes, in the jar, thank you . . . and if I *don't* make enough bread for my customers there'll be big trouble, big trouble, there'll be angry crowds hammering on the door, 'Give us the bread, Miah, give us the bread, or we'll chop off your head!' Seriously, we'll have to hide in the cupboard whilst they kick the door in and turn the place upside down . . .

> *Josip stops what he is doing.*
> *Mr Miah carries on for a moment, unaware.*
> *Meanwhile, Anna enters, sees Grandmother is apparently asleep, and reaches up easily for the photograph. She looks at Grandmother again and puts the photograph in an apron pocket. She starts plaiting her hair in the mirror.*

Mr Miah (*noticing that Josip has gone quiet*) What's the matter?

Josip Nothing . . .

Mr Miah Sure?

Josip (*brief pause*) I hide in cupboard three days. When *politz* come to my house. They take my mother and father away . . . (*He repeats this in his own language.*) *Orum beede tre ditch. An politz domun bin.*

Mr Miah (*brief pause*) I see. (*Brief pause.*) Anything else?

Josip Nothing . . . no . . .

Mr Miah Very well. So, this is how we do it, Josip, you can sprinkle the spice gently into the dough, like this . . .

They begin.

Anna (*quietly*) Grandma Eva?

Grandma opens her eyes.

Grandmother How's the dough, Anna, has it risen yet?

Grandmother goes to get it.
She is suddenly aware of Anna's hair.

What have you done to your hair?

Anna Nothing, I just thought I'd . . .

Grandmother It doesn't matter, it doesn't matter. I . . .

Anna Grandma can we go to the train station?

Grandmother Train station? Whatever for? Your apron, please, help me knock back the dough.

Anna (*putting apron on*) Grandma, what was your home like?

Grandmother My *home*?

Anna Yes, where you grew up . . .

Grandmother Can't remember . . .

Anna Oh . . . Where was it, far away?

Grandmother Not so far, but far enough.

Anna Don't you want to go back . . .

Grandmother Why? I should want to go back after all this time?

Anna Is *this* your home? . . .

Grandmother (*stops and looks at Anna again. Points to her heart*) This is home, Anna, you are my home. What on earth is the matter with you, mmm?

> *Grandmother goes to her. She touches Anna's hair briefly. They hug.*

Josip How long you been here?

Mr Miah A long time, I forget, I was young, now I'm old, *beshi boysh* . . .

Josip You go home?

Mr Miah Me?

Josip Why you no go home?

Mr Miah *Desh, bidesh* . . .

Josip *Desh*?

Mr Miah *Desh*, 'home'. *Bidesh*, 'away'. *Desh*, *bidesh*, which is which?

Josip You go back?

Mr Miah *Hoyto*. Maybe, one day.

Josip Where your home before?

Mr Miah My home before? Across the seven seas and far away.

Josip Why you come here?

Mr Miah (*busy*) Why I came is a secret and a long story.

Josip Why you come here?

Mr Miah It is not considered polite to ask too many questions.

> *Looks at Josip and notices his injury.*

What have you done to your head?

Josip Nothing . . .

Mr Miah Let me . . .

Josip Is okay . . .

Mr Miah Let me see . . .

> *Mr Miah takes off the apron and goes to Josip.*
> *Grandmother is still aware that Anna's hair is*
> *different from usual. She breaks the embrace.*
> *Mr Miah is now carefully examining Josip's head.*

Grandmother Don't put your hair like that, it's not right.

Anna Why?

Grandmother Nothing . . . (*She picks up the utensils*
that Mr Miah just put down.) Now, wash your hands
please, come and help me. (*She resumes bread-making.*)

Anna Do I have to?

Grandmother Yes.

Anna Grandma, did you come by train?

Grandmother Train?

Anna From your home?

Grandmother When?

Anna When you were a girl, did you come by train?

Grandmother Train, yes, boat, yes, why? What's with
trains all of a sudden, will you please give me a hand?

Anna Oh! Oh! What's this, in my pocket? (*Produces the*
photograph.) Grandma, that's strange, I didn't notice it
before, I wonder where it's come from . . .

Grandmother Come on, I've nearly finished . . .

Anna Who *is* this, Grandma? Who's this lady, is this you, Grandma?

Pause.

Grandmother Where did you get that from?

Anna It fell out, from the cupboard, I mean, you must . . .

Grandmother *Give* it to me please . . .

Anna You must have dropped it or something, and put it in your apron pocket, um, who *are* these people? . . .

Grandmother (*angry*) Give it to me, *now* . . .

Anna Who are they?

Grandmother Give me the photograph! (*Takes it.*)

Anna Who was she? . . .

Grandmother stares at her angrily. Then she returns to the chair, sits and closes her eyes, holding the photograph.

Grandma, who was she?

Mr Miah (*getting some ointment*) Did you do this at school?

Josip shrugs.

Josip, answer me, please . . .

Josip shrugs.

Fighting again?

Josip No . . .

Mr Miah Kick-boxing ?

Josip Yes, yes, I remember . . .

Mr Miah Josip, how did this happen?

Josip I fell. Ow!! (*in response to ointment*)

Mr Miah Keep still . . .

Anna Grandma . . .?

Mr Miah Come on, we have to sort this out.

Josip No, please . . .

Anna Grandma . . .?

Whistle. Sound of steam train leaving station.

Josip Please, Mr Miah, it was accident – (*going*) My fault . . . Mr Miah, no trouble, please . . .

Repeat of whistle, sound of steam train leaving station.

SCENE SEVEN: EARLIER

Banging on the wall.
Grandmother enters as a girl, aged twelve or thirteen, carrying a small leather suitcase and a paper parcel.
Official 1 enters.
He looks at her.

Grandmother Excuse me, please. Is this right place?

Repeat of steam train.

Official 1 Sit down, sit down, er Eva? . . .

Grandmother (*quietly*) Thank you.

Official 1 Make yourself comfortable.

Grandmother Thank you. My . . . sister . . .

Official 1 This won't take long.

Grandmother Thank you. My sister . . . outside . . .

Official 1 May I offer you a cup of tea?

Grandmother Thank you, but . . .

Official 1 How do you take your tea?

Grandmother Excuse, please?

Official 1 How do you drink your tea, *with* or *without*?

Grandmother Excuse, please, not good I'm speaking . . .

Official 1 How . . . do . . . you . . . drink . . . your . . . tea?

Grandmother Tea is . . . tea.

Official 1 (*writes*) Applicant answered: 'Tea is tea.' (*He smiles.*)

Grandmother May I please . . . have . . . a glass water?

Official 1 (*writing*) Applicant requested 'a glass of water'. Now, where have you come from, Eva?

She hands over boat/train tickets, and another document.

(*cursory look*) Yes. Yes. Terrible business. (*He looks at her.*) My sympathies. Naturally. And why have you come here?

Grandmother tenses. A memory. She doesn't look at him.

Official 1 Why have you come *here*? As opposed to, say . . . somewhere else?

Grandmother Here because . . .

Official 1 Yes?

Grandmother Because . . .

Official 1 Yes? . . .

Grandmother Because nowhere else to go . . .

Official 1 (*doubtful but not unpleasant*) Really?

Grandmother – puzzled, apprehensive – shrugs.

(*writing on the form*) This won't take much longer, I'm so sorry to take up your time like this . . .

Grandmother smiles, still uncertain.

We have to be careful, you see, who comes in, who stays. It's a tricky business, very delicate, a balancing act, and we can't be too careful. (*Looks up.*) I'm sure you understand . . .

Grandmother Yes, yes . . .

Official 1 (*signs a paper*) Well, that will be all. For now. (*returning documents and giving an address*) Here's an address to go to for tonight, it's a bakery so you'll find it warm and cosy, No 15 on the left-hand side.

Official is already going.

Good luck, young lady. And welcome on behalf of the Emperor and the people . . .

He is going.

Grandmother Thank you, but . . .

Official 1 Yes? . . .

Official is exiting.
Sound of whistle again.
Josip arrives, angry. He goes to the mirror and starts practising kick-boxing in front of it.

Grandmother My sister . . . What will happen to sister?

Official has gone.
Steam train departs station.
Music.

SCENE EIGHT: NOW MEETS THEN

*In the following scene the characters have very clear
pathways through the space. Some of these coincide with
each other, others are 'distinctive'.*

Grandmother exits.

*Anna arrives and goes to the dough. She starts
shaping it.*

Josip leaves the mirror and goes to the dough.

Anna leaves the dough and goes to the mirror.

Josip flattens the dough in his anger.

*Anna performs a brief exaggerated version of her
mirror antics, then returns to the dough to that find it
has been moved and changed in shape. She looks around
her slowly, then shrugs it off.*

*Josip has passed her on the way, and now performs a
brief exaggerated nodding and shaking parody of himself
in the mirror. He revolves the mirror through 360 degrees
and returns to the dough.*

*Anna returns to the mirror, and finds herself caught
up in Josip's nodding and shaking action. She revolves
the mirror through 360 degrees.*

*Josip finds the dough has changed and looks around
him slowly, then shrugs it off.*

Anna Grandma . . .?

Josip senses something and goes towards the mirror.

Josip Mr Miah?

*Josip is caught up in Anna's mirror action, revolves
the mirror again, then tears himself away.*

*Anna has sensed something, picks up the dough
and carries it around the room as if it was a
dangerous object.*

Josip has taken the dough from her without realising it.
Music.
They are both aware of an unseen force in the room, and try to take charge of the dough, the mirror, the space.
Finally, Anna slowly cimbs through the mirror.
They see each other.

Anna (*screaming, calling off*) Grandma!

Josip (*screaming*) Baba! Mama!

Anna Grandma!!

They run around the room in terror, but cannot escape from each other. Pause.

What . . . are . . . you . . . doing?

Josip *Ho viche Josip, en vazdec du?*

Anna Leave me alone or I'll call the police.

Josip (*nodding his head*) *Ne* . . . (*shaking his head*) No, please, no *politz* . . . *Ne politz,* is okay, is okay, *ne politz.*

Pause.

Anna What are you doing with my grandmother's bread?

Josip I . . . *making* bread, what you do?

Anna Excuse me!

Josip Excuse please?

Anna How did you get in here?

Josip Through door, how you?

Anna I was here already. Where's Grandma?

Josip Who?

Anna Where's my grandmother?

Josip I not know 'granmother' . . .

Anna What have you *done* with my grandma?

Josip (*shrugs, showing dough.*) I make to eat . . .

Anna (*shocked*) Oh my God . . . you're a werewolf . . .
you're a werewolf and you've eaten my grandma!
Grandma! Grandma! (*Picks up a heavy object as a
weapon.*)

Josip Wolf? Wolf, yes, I know 'Little . . . Red . . .
Hiding . . . ' Good story, I know this story from my
country. '*Rojo Capon Itse.*' Ha ha, me a werewolf, ha
ha ha!

Anna Stop it! How did you get in?

Josip I been here for hour. Where you come from? Door
shut, I always locking door on my own. Ha ha, me
werewolf. (*Howls.*) 'Ahooooooow!!'

Anna Stop it!

Josip 'Ahooooooow!!'

Anna Stop it!

   Pause.

Josip You ghost?

Anna That's not funny.

Josip You a ghost in my kitchen, *dazvitsa rojde.* ['*The
devil get rid of you.*']

Anna There are no ghosts, silly . . .

Josip Yes, yes, big ghosts in my country, stories from
forests, I know is true . . .

Anna I'm real, you're the ghost if there is one . . .

Josip I think, no. (*Pinches himself.*) Ow, no, I no ghost.

Anna How do you know?

Josip It hurt, that's how! Let me see if you a ghost . . .

Anna No, don't touch me or I'll scream!

Josip It's okay, it's okay, I just touch arm . . .

Slight pause.

Anna Very well . . .

Josip (*touching her arm gently. She flinches*) No, you real, I real . . .

Anna But the door was locked.

Josip Why you mess about with my bread?

Anna I beg your pardon?

Josip Every time I put . . . stuff . . . er . . . duff . . .

Anna Dough . . .

Josip Dough stuff, down it move . . .

Anna Same here.

Josip I know something strange this place, I know ghosts something, or just other people this place at other time, back forward, er, pasts, future, innit . . .

Anna That's what my grandma said.

Josip She say . . . ?

Anna She said she could smell other people's cooking in the oven, as if it was still fresh, like they were spirits in the same place, making different things but belonging here just the same.

Josip (*goes to oven*) Is maybe, I dunno . . . sssh!

Anna (*joins him listening at the oven door*) What?

Josip Sssh, I hearing something, listen: 'Let me out, let me out of wolf, help help, he cook me up for eating baddy wolf.' (*Jumps up at her.*) 'Ahoooooooow!! Ahoooooooow!!'

Anna Stop it!

Josip Ha ha ha ha! So what your name?

Anna What's yours?

Josip Josip, I tell already.

Anna Why can't you talk properly? Where do you come from anyway?

Josip Nowhere.

Anna You can't come from nowhere . . .

Josip Yes, I boy from nowhere . . .

Anna (*playful*) Alright, smartypants, this is my home, not yours, I don't know where you come from, I don't know *when* you come from, and I don't care, because I want you out before I call the police, understand, you've . . . outstayed your welcome . . .

Josip No *politz* . . .

Grandmother (*from off*) Anna?

Anna Go away . . .

Josip How? I here, *you* going some place . . .

Anna Go away, she mustn't see you . . .

Josip Where I go, how I go? Okay, try mirror, make ghost magics . . .

They are both caught between turning the mirror and constantly reshaping the dough according to how they think it should be.

Mr Miah (*from off*) Josip!

Grandmother (*from off*) Anna?

Josip Mr Miah?

They look in the mirror again but can't see each other.

Anna?

Anna Josip? (*pronounced incorrectly*)

Josip exits, looking around him as he goes. Anna looks around her.

Josip . . .?

Music.

SCENE NINE: THEN AND NOW

In silence, Grandmother enters and goes to the table, puts on the apron and gets the baking tray ready.
Anna gets the dough out. She daren't say anything.
Grandmother makes four long sausages of dough on the bread board. She starts plaiting the strips of dough.
She starts to sing her niggun.
She stops, overcome.

Grandmother One piece for each of us. Plaited like hair and holding each other for ever.

Anna I'm sorry I took your photo, Grandma.

Grandmother Things were very bad. My parents put us . . . my sister . . . (*She wipes her hands and produces the photograph.*)

Anna Sister?

Grandmother This is her here, look, I can see you in her already even though she's a little older.

Anna Why . . .?

Grandmother Why what, darling?

Anna Why were things bad?

Grandmother Well, that's all history now, I was scared, they just put us on the train.

Sound of steam train, whistles.
    Grandmother takes Anna's hand. They become the young sisters at the station.

Father takes the photograph at the station. Mother is holding all her feelings in – look, see how tightly she is holding on to her handbag. Look at her face, lips all tight, she knows what's going to happen.

Anna But they're both smiling, why are they smiling? I want to cry . . .

Grandmother Sssh, Anna, smile for the camera. Smile for Mama and Papa.

Anna Why can't they come with us?

Grandmother It's not allowed, don't cry yet, wait till we go into the tunnel, then we can cry.

Sound ceases. She continues plaiting the dough.

Now . . . you have to be very careful with the dough now, or it will come out all wrong . . . and then the stories won't come out right will they?

Anna Your sister, what was her name? Why have you never told me about her?

Grandmother Her name was Anna. Like you. Did I never tell you? Just like you . . .

Silence.

It was her birthday, the twenty-seventh. I hate the twenty-seventh. We left in such a hurry that we left her papers behind, her passport, I can see it now sitting on the table by the front door . . .

Sound of horses and carriages, maybe a tram.

. . . on a small dark table next to an elephant-foot hat-stand, she gives them to me so she can do up the buttons on her coat. 'It's a cold day, Anna, do your coat up, give me your passport, I'll hold it for you.' But I put the passport down by mistake just as we're leaving, and I forget it, it's my fault we leave her passport behind . . . Father says, 'Have you got everything?' as he closes the door. It's my fault. It's my fault . . .

Sound ceases.

See, what a story for this loaf of bread, eh?

Anna What happened?

Grandmother What happened was, when we got here my Anna didn't have her passport, so . . . they sent her back. It was my fault, Anna . . .

Sound ceases.

Anna Sent her back? What *happened* to her when they sent her back? Grandma?

Grandmother repeats her earlier action of smelling something else in the oven as she opens it.

Grandmother Sometimes I can feel ghosts here, not unhappy ghosts like my sister or my parents, but people who've been in this room before, maybe even in the future, yes, that's quite possible . . .

Anna The future . . .?

Mr Miah passes through with a bowl of steaming rice. He stands eating it in front of Grandmother, but they are oblivious to each other.

Grandmother Sometimes as I open the oven I can smell strange fragrances, strange aromas, as if other people are using the oven to bake bread when I'm not looking, sometimes other smells, cooking smells, cooking from the heart of a family, delicate rice, roasting potatoes, but mostly bread, other people's bread, and it feels as if someone is always in my shadow, and I'm in theirs . . .

Anna Well, actually . . .

Grandmother (*to Anna*) . . . and when I bake the story bread for you, child, when we break the bread open, there are other stories I didn't know about, as if someone has slipped something into the yeast, and strangely enough, Anna, what the ghosts put into my bread is what makes it taste so good, but then . . . I expect I'm getting old, I'm losing my marbles . . .

Anna Grandma . . .

Josip enters, kick-boxing noisily and goes to the mirror. Grandmother is unaware of him.

(*to Josip*) What are you doing here?

Josip reacts.

Grandmother I'm trying to finish this bread, if only you'll let me . . .

Anna (*to Grandmother*) No, I mean, oh, no, it's alright, Grandma . . . (*to Josip*) Go away, will you? . . .

Grandmother Pardon!

Josip is still kick-boxing around the room. He makes his way to Grandmother, who can't see or hear him.

Anna No, I . . . mean . . .

Josip moves something out of Grandmother's way.

Grandma . . .

Grandmother What? I'm sure I just . . . you see all these memories just upset and confuse me, some things one shouldn't talk about . . .

Josip picks up a bag of flour and puts his hand in, preparing to toss flour over her.

Anna No!

Grandmother (*glazes bread with egg and adds poppy seeds prior to baking*) No what . . . ?

Anna Don't, please . . .

Grandmother What do you mean, 'Don't'? If I don't put it in now, it'll go dry.

She bends down to the oven. Josip throws flour all over her.

What *are* you doing, child!

Anna Nothing, it wasn't me . . .

Grandmother Don't lie to me! . . .

Josip puffs flour out of the bag, as if there is a mouse inside.

No, no, not a mouse, please! Where is it, Anna, not a mouse, please . . .

They both stand on chairs and scream. Josip does the same. Then he makes as if to break an egg on Grandmother's head.

Anna No!! Please don't . . .

Grandmother What's happening?

Josip teases Anna with the egg over Grandmother's head.

Anna (*laughs despite herself*) Stop it! . . .

Josip smashes the egg over Grandmother's head.

Josip Ahooooow!! Ahoooooooow!!

Grandmother can't believe she has been covered in raw egg. She goes to pick up a tea towel to wipe herself down, but Josip makes it float across the room and dances it around Grandmother. She stands stock-still.

Anna Stop it! (*Laughs.*) Stop it now Josip!

Josip She can't see me, she can't see me . . .

Anna No . . . Stop it . . .

Josip Ahoooooow!

Everything subsides as they look at Grandmother.
She wipes herself down, removes the apron and goes to the mirror to straighten up. She stares into the mirror. After a moment she returns to the bread as if nothing had happened. Anna and Josip look at each other.
Josip goes closer and mirrors all her actions, like a shadow.
Anna giggles. Grandmother is apparently oblivious to Josip.
Then she grabs Josip.

PETER RUMNEY

Grandmother Got you!

The children scream and scream.
Sound of an ocean-going vessel and tugs docking.

Act Three

SCENE TEN: BETWEEN NOW AND THEN

Sound of knocking on the wall.

Mr Miah, younger, makes an entry through the wall, in a similar manner to the others earlier, but with less apparent effort.

It has been raining. He has an umbrella.

Mr Miah (*to audience*) Fifty years ago I step ashore in promised land. I have been at sea for many months. I am not yet steady on my feet. Why do I remember this today?

Officials 2 and 3 arrive. They wear campaign medals.

Official 2 Ah, Mr Miah . . . Raining again? You'll have to get used to our damp weather, I'm afraid.

Mr Miah In my country it rains non-stop for three months every year. Also, I have been at sea for three years, where, of course, the water is extremely damp indeed.

Official 2 Yes, of course . . .

Official 3 We have carefully considered your application, Mr Miah. There are just a few questions before we can make any decision as to whether you may stay in our country, do you understand?

Mr Miah Yes, yes, of course I understand.

Official 2 Good . . . (*Looks at Official 3.*)

Official 3 Mr Miah, you have done great service to the Empire during the war. I see from your file that, like my colleague here, in fact, you were awarded the Emperor's Gold Medal for bravery.

Mr Miah produces the medal in a box.

Mr Miah Yes, yes, it was an honour to serve the Emperor at sea.

Official 3 And without – yes, congratulations – without your . . . contribution to the war effort, and the contribution of your fellow countrymen, we could not have survived and triumphed . . .

Mr Miah Yes, madam. Many men of my village died fighting for the Emperor in the war. Many drowned at sea. Without such a medal. Already nobody remembers this, which I am thinking is perhaps a shame all in all.

Official 3 (*looking at a document*) We note that you have been offered work, at least of a temporary nature, for, I believe, six months, is that correct?

Mr Miah Yes, madam, I have been offered work. I can start at the bakery this evening if you give me . . . 'green light'.

Official 2 We also note, however, that you have a large family, many relatives relying on you at . . . er, home, your . . . country of origin. Parents, uncles, cousins, people like that . . .

Mr Miah (*delighted, produces photographs to show*) Yes, yes, I'm afraid these photos are a little old, of course – my . . . nephew, my brother, my . . . beloved parents . . .

Official 3 (*ignoring photographs*) Are you intending to bring all these people to this country?

Mr Miah is puzzled.

Official 3 Are you intending to bring your family here to stay? There is only so much work, land, food, Mr Miah. There must be a limit to the Emperor's generosity . . .

(*Smiles.*) You are a man of the sea, Mr Miah – we cannot allow the 'tide' to come in and drown our land, can we?

Mr Miah No no no no. I myself intend to stay, only for a very short time, perhaps, a year or two at most, before returning to my village, to my people. I will be a guest merely, a hard-working guest here, my *hands* will be busy here, my *heart* will be busy at home . . .

(*to audience*) Josip's letter will come today. Why do I think of the past? Why do I recall the day I arrived? Because Josip's letter comes today. The new Emperor's decision.

The Officials leave.
  Mr Miah finalises his dough in preparation for baking.

I have helped to make this country, in my small way. I was a stranger, now I am at home. I have been in this land for nearly fifty years. I came, I stayed, I made bread, spice bread like my father. *Allahi tandre behesh nosib horoka.* I stayed, ten years became twenty, until I no longer knew where home was, *desh, bidesh.* I lost touch with my family, life slipped through my fingers, but this was home. Nowadays a stranger is no longer welcome in this place. If I arrived here today they would not let me in. And the new Emperor would never taste the delights of my spiced bread.

Mr Miah puts the letter in a prominent position.

No . . . I cannot open it. I'm afraid of what it will say.

Josip enters. He kick-boxes at the mirror.
  Grandmother enters and goes to the table.

SCENE ELEVEN: THEN AND NOW

Grandmother puts her bread in the oven to cook.
  Mr Miah puts his bread in the oven to cook.

Grandmother Have another piece of toast, Josip, try the cherry jam.

Mr Miah exits.

Josip Thank you, Grandmother lady.

Grandmother Tomorrow I'll make bread from your country, Josip, the flat bread. I found a recipe in the library. It won't be the same as your mother . . . Well, I'll try to make it, do my best to make you feel at home.

Josip's music is heard.
  Josip has stopped eating. He is very still.
  Grandmother looks at him.
  Anna enters.

Hello, Anna.

Anna Can I have some toast, please?

Grandmother It's nearly dinner time.

Anna But Josip's having some . . .

Grandmother Just a small piece then.

Anna That's not fair, he's taken the last two cherries, there's only runny stuff left . . .

Josip Sorry, Anna, I have enough now.

Grandmother I can make some more tomorrow.

Anna That's not fair . . .

Josip Have some mine.

Anna No thanks, it's got your spit on it . . .

Josip I cut off for you, is plenty for both.

Anna I don't want your spitty toast, Josip . . .

Grandmother Anna!

Anna It's not hygienic . . .

Josip Why you stroppy, Anna?

Anna It's not *hygienic*, smartypants, it's not clean, it's got germs on it. I don't want toast with someone else's germs on it.

Josip I go back to Mr Miah's time easy if you no want me, I go back now, Grandmother . . .

Grandmother I'm sorry, Josip, Anna *does* want you to come here as often as you like.

Anna No, I don't . . .

Grandmother Visit us through the mirror whenever you like . . .

Anna Whose side are you on, Grandma?

Grandmother I'm not on anybody's side.

Anna Anyone would think *he* belongs here, not me. *You* don't know how to make story bread, *do* you, so *you* don't belong here . . .

Grandmother Anna!

Josip I can learn quick make story bread, I show you. I also making spice bread with Mr Miah, same place, same cooker, stupid-panties . . .

Anna Stupid yourself . . .

Grandmother Anna, stop it now.

Anna Why . . .

Grandmother Because I . . .

Anna I don't want to stop, you can't make me stop. I'm not a baby, and you're not my parents . . .

Grandmother That's enough!

Anna No, if I say anything you just tell me to be quiet! This is my home and I don't want to share it with anyone else, I don't want a stupid 'boy from nowhere' in here messing up my things and spoiling them, and then I get the blame for the mess . . .

Grandmother No you don't . . .

Anna Yes I do, it's always like that, you tell me to behave like an adult, but you don't treat me like an adult, you treat me like a baby . . .

Josip I'm sorry I in your way, Anna. I go now, Gran'ma.

Grandmother You're not in her way . . .

Anna She's not your 'gran'ma', she's not your grandma!

Grandmother Anna . . .

Anna You've stolen my grandma, you nasty foreign boy!

Grandmother Anna, that's enough . . .

Anna No . . .

Grandmother *Will* you let me *speak* . . . ?

Anna No, you let *me* speak, I hate you, both of you . . .

Grandmother Stop it . . .

Anna No, you stop it . . .

Josip *Please, stop* . . .

Grandmother Don't interfere, Josip, we have to sort this out.

Josip Please, both you two . . .

Anna You both think you're so special because you got kicked out from somewhere else, because you had a hard time and lost your parents, you think I've got to be nice to you both because you've had a hard time, but I don't, this is my place, *my* place . . .

> *Sound of aircraft landing, as before.*
> *Grandmother is very still.*
> *The sound of harsh voices, as before.*

Josip (*as at beginning of the play*) I am . . . boy from nowhere . . .

> *Anna kicks out.*
> *The sound of the window breaking, as before,*
> *repeatedly.*

Grandmother Anna!

> *Anna going to the oven, opens it, burns herself,*
> *appears to tip the bread out on the floor.*

Anna I hate your stupid story bread . . .

Grandmother (*picking it up*) Stop that, you ungrateful child . . .

Anna What for? I didn't ask to be your granddaughter, I didn't ask to be here, nobody asked me, I didn't want to be dumped here with you and your horrid grey hair and stupid precious story bread . . .

Grandmother That's enough, *now!*

Anna No!

Josip Please, *odvitze nam, vitze*, please . . .

Grandmother Anna . . .

Anna No . . .

*Mr Miah enters and goes straight to the mirror,
oblivious to the others.*

Josip Please, both you two . . .

*Mr Miah removes his campaign medal from its box
and pins it on himself.*

I fank you for letting me be here. I know is difficult.
Please, I not bein' rude, please, I fank you, but I did not
want to come 'ere. I did not want to come 'ere dis
country. I wanta be in my home an' appy. I not come
from 'nowhere' . . . Is sad, yeah? My joke, I try forget
where I come from, the badness, I try to forget the music
of my fahvver and the cooking of my muvver, if I 'ear
the music I jus' cry, if I smell the food I jus' cry, but my
heart still is there, I leave everything behind, I bring
nuffingk, I shamed I bring nuffingk to give, but I 'ad to
come, there nowhere else to go, so I do best I can to be
not 'ere, invisible, not make trouble, but I cannot go
back, if I go back I swallowed up by grey cold cloud,
it squeeze my life away, it choke me like it choke my
family, if I not wanted here I go other place, I don't
know where . . .

Josip cries.
    Grandmother goes to Josip.
    Anna exits.
    Mr Miah goes to the table and sits.
    He places the letter in front of him.

SCENE TWELVE: THEN VISITS NOW

Josip and Grandmother leave.
   Anna goes to the mirror. She plaits her hair.

Mr Miah Some people say that everything is possible. That the power is here. In our imaginations, and in our hands. Others say that the power is above. That what will be will be.

   He reads the letter.
      He washes his hands in a ritual fashion.
      He sings.
      Mr Miah stops singing.
      Anna picks up a musical strand from Mr Miah or sings Grandmother's song.
      They exchange musical motifs, apparently unaware of each other.
      Then Anna goes to sit down at the table.
      She looks at Mr Miah.
      He stops singing.

Anna I'm sorry, I didn't mean to interrupt you, sir.

Mr Miah You are welcome here, young lady.

Anna I came through the . . .

Mr Miah *Ami dehsi . . .* I see . . .

   Pause.

Anna Have you been crying?

Mr Miah It is considered impolite to ask too many questions.

Anna I haven't asked you any yet.

Mr Miah True.

Anna Adults only want to answer questions when it suits them.

Mr Miah Perhaps also true.

Anna Adults only want us to ask the questions that they want to answer.

Mr Miah True again. I assume you've come to find out what will happen to Josip?

Anna No! I've come to get away from them.

Mr Miah I see.

Anna Two's company, three's a crowd.

Mr Miah I know.

Anna Grandma doesn't want to talk to me any more, she just sits there waiting for Josip to come through the mirror, then she stuffs him with food, and talks to him instead of me. She's not interested in anything I have to say any more, it's all: 'Poor Josip, just a minute, Anna, have some more toast, Josip, finish *all* the jam, have *two* spoonfuls of sugar in your tea, how do you like your tea, Josip, is it too hot is it too cold for you . . .?'

Pause.

Mr Miah Can I offer you some tea . . . Anna?

Anna No, thank you.

Pause.

What will happen to Josip?

Mr Miah He will be sent back. The Emperor's police will come for him soon, maybe next week, and send him back, they will take him to the airport and send him back . . .

Anna Why . . . ?

Mr Miah Why? They do not believe his story. They think he is making it up. They do not believe he is in danger or frightened. They believe he is only here for the 'jam', Anna. They believe he is here because he wants your jam.

Anna What do you think, Mr Miah?

Mr Miah (*getting up from the table*) I think I must make my bread, or I will have angry customers. I have a busy night ahead. I will need to speak with Josip. At some point. Not yet. If you will excuse me.

> *He goes to the mirror, removes his medal and puts it in the box.*

Anna Mr Miah, I brought you a present, some honey to put on your bread . . .
  I don't know if it goes with spice bread . . .

> *She puts it on the table and goes to the oven to check the bread.*
>   *Josip enters in high spirits, kick-boxing.*

(*oblivious to Josip*) Grandma's story bread . . . Mr Miah's spice bread . . . (*breathing in the aromas*) Mmmmmm!

> *Anna exits.*
>   *Mr Miah is waiting to tell Josip.*

SCENE THIRTEEN: NOW

Josip Awright, Mr Miah, awright! . . .

Mr Miah You're late, Josip, it's nearly half past . . .

Josip Safe, safe, Mr Miah, we missed the bus, right?

Mr Miah Who is 'we', Josip?

Josip Jim, Devern, Iqbal, we 'ad such a larf, Mr Miah, right, this boy from Year 9, right, let off a stink bomb on the bus, right, and we was like throwin' up and laughin', right, and the bus driver come upstairs and say, 'What's goin' on then?', and I say, 'Nuffink, mate,' and he looks at me and says, 'Where *you* come from then, sunshine?' And then Iqbal say, 'He's coming from the bakery, No 15 on the left-hand side, innit,' and Devern he say, 'Dwan warry 'bout 'im, man, he de buoy fram noweair,' then we jump off the bus and we run, laughin', laughin', I fell over laughin' . . .

Sound of children laughing in stairwell.

My friends, they're safe, Mr Miah, innit . . .

Mr Miah Josip . . .

Josip Yes, Mr Miah?

Pause.

Mr Miah I have some bad news . . .

Music.

SCENE FOURTEEN: NOW AND FOR EVER

At the beginning of this scene each performer will move through a series or 'loop' of actions, which repeats itself and/or develops as a ritual meal is set on the stage.

The sense is of very individual people's experiences running concurrently but separately in the space, with moments of essential contact with other characters, usually with an object as the intermediary.

Grandmother, then Mr Miah, then Josip appear through the wall, exactly as they did earlier in the play.

The table is gradually laid for a feast.

This action loop has the sense of being created, broken down and created again.

The following loop is roughly what happened in the first production:
Anna lays place settings for her and Grandmother, opposite each other.
Mr Miah lays for himself at right angles to them.
Grandmother arranges and places a chair.
Anna sits.
Mr Miah lays a place setting for Josip.
Josip takes up the fourth space and sits.
Josip smiles at Anna.
They are all coming together.
Anna removes Josip's place setting angrily and leaves the table.
Josip leaves the table.
Mr Miah lays a place setting for Josip, and so on.
Finally, after approximately four loops, the table is set, with candles, breads, etc.
Mr Miah brings spice bread to the table.
Grandmother brings story bread to the table.
Anna brings flat bread to the table.
Josip is standing alone.
They look at Josip.
He shakes his head slowly.
Anna goes to him.
He nods his head slowly and joins them at the table.
They wash hands in a ritual fashion.
They light candles in a ritual fashion.
They sit.
Grandmother invites Josip to break open the story bread.

Grandmother Why do we break the bread with our hands, Anna?

Anna So as not to kill the stories, Grandma.

Grandmother And why do we eat the bread whilst it is still warm?

Anna To give us the warmth of life.

Mr Miah invites Anna to break open or cut the spice bread.

Mr Miah Josip, why do I tear the bread like this?

Josip So the spices can fill our home with richness, Mr Miah.

Josip offers the spice bread round.

Mr Miah And what do the spices remind us of, young man?

Anna (*puts her hand up*) I know, I know, Mr Miah!

Grandmother (*smiling*) Anna!

Mr Miah Yes, Anna?

Pause.

Anna What was the question? I forgot, sorry . . .

Mr Miah What do the spices remind us of, Anna?

Anna The spices remind you of your home, *bidesh*, I mean, *desh* . . . and they are the richness of what you brought to this land.

Josip (*nods*) Desh, bidesh . . .

Anna (*apologetic*) But I still don't like the taste, I'm afraid . . .

Mr Miah Anna, let me tell you a little secret. I don't like bread at all, never touch the stuff, much prefer rice . . .

Anna But you're a baker!

Mr Miah (*shrugs*) *Ham, hamu,* a job's a job!

> *Brief loud knocking from the 'front door'.*

Josip What's the time?

Mr Miah They're early.

Anna No!

> *Grandmother gets up from the table, walks towards the 'front door' and calls off.*

Grandmother Go away! It's not time yet. Go away and leave us in peace! (*She returns to the table.*) Come on. We must eat . . .

> *They eat in silence for a moment.*
> *Knocking from the street.*
> *They begin eating as if their lives depend on it.*
> *Knocking.*
> *They stop.*
> *Knocking stops.*

Josip I get my bag, Mr Miah.

Anna I'll help you.

Josip (*hint of accusation*) No. I'm on my own now, innit.

> *Silence. Anna is crying.*

Okay, yeah, you help me, Anna.

> *Josip and Anna exit to get his bag from within.*

Grandmother (*looking at the photograph of her and Anna as children*) Well, Mr Miah . . . ?

Mr Miah Some people say that everything is possible, madam. That the power is here. In our imaginations, and in our hands. Others say that the power is above. That what will be will be.

Knocking.
  Grandmother sings quietly.
  She moves the cooker and table as if to block
  ingress from the street.

Grandmother Come on, it's help I'm needing, not an audience . . .

Mr Miah helps her with the barricade.
  Knocking stops.

Mr Miah, whatever happens, look after Anna for me, yes?

Mr Miah (*brief pause*) Yes, madam . . .

Intermittent knocking where appropriate.
  Sound/music underneath the dialogue.

Anna (*off*) Grandma, Grandma!

Grandmother Good, lock the front door . . .

Anna and Josip are entering with a small bag.
  Mr Miah goes out to check the 'front door'.

Anna Grandma, Grandma, there's people fighting, down in the street . . . they're trying to stop the Emperor's men from coming up the stairs . . .

Josip Mr Miah . . . ?

Anna Grandma, what are you doing?

Grandmother Josip, come here . . .

Mr Miah returns.

Josip Mr Miah . . . *Baba?* Dad? . . . Dad?

Anna Grandma . . .

Grandmother Come on, Josip, they'll have to take me first, get under the table – quickly!

Anna Grandma, what are you doing? . . .

Grandmother (*pushing Josip under the table, then getting on the top*) They'll have to take me first! If they want to take Josip, they'll have to take me first . . . I may be losing my marbles, Anna, but I'm not losing another child to the Emperor's men. If anything happens to me, Mr Miah will look after you . . .

Anna Grandma, please, they'll take you too, Grandma, they'll take both of you . . .

Josip (*comes out from under the table*) Dad? Dad? Stop Grandmother lady, please . . . Dad, stop her please . . .

Grandmother (*as Mr Miah is embracing Josip, then returning him to Grandmother*) Don't say anything, Josip . . . I should have done this for my sister fifty years ago. We'll show them . . . Come on now . . .

Grandmother pushes Josip under the table again.

Anna Stop it, Grandma, stop it . . .

Anna tries to stop Grandmother standing on the table. They tussle.
    Grandmother embraces Anna, then pushes her towards Mr Miah.

Grandmother I love you, Anna . . . Go with Mr Miah. I should have done this for my sister . . .

Anna What about me, Grandma? What's going to happen to me?

Mr Miah pulls Anna away from the barricade and back to safety.

What about me, Grandma . . . ?

Mr Miah The power is here, in our hands and in our imaginations . . .

Mr Miah pins on his medal.
  Knocking and banging.
  Grandmother sings as she stands on the barricade.
  She brandishes the photograph.
  Mr Miah joins them at the barricade and sings.
He is trying both to support Grandmother and to keep an eye on Anna.
  Josip sings from under the table.
  Knocking and banging.

Anna Grandma, the Emperor's men . . .

Grandmother Come on then, come and get me if you dare!

Anna The Emperor's men . . .

Grandmother This is for you, too, Anna.

Anna . . . they'll take you, Grandma, not just Josip! They'll take you too, Grandma! Grandma . . .

Grandmother (*to the Emperor's men*) Come on then, *komma dee hier* . . .

Anna Grandma, please, come down, Mr Miah, Josip, what am I going to do? What's going to happen to me?

  Josip comes out from under the table and starts dancing and gesticulating in the direction of the 'front door'.
  Grandmother is gesticulating and shouting on the table top.
  Mr Miah and Josip are singing and dancing defiantly.

Grandmother Come on then, you lot, *vechez hoch damin,* come and take him away, come and take him if you dare!

Anna Grandma, what am I going to do . . . ?

Grandmother *Komma dee hier en vechez hoch damin!*

Anna Grandma! . . . Grandma! . . .

The Emperor's men arrive.
The sound of breaking glass, very loud and close.

The End.

Children's Theatre Companies

Act One Theatre Company
281 Luton Road, Harpenden, Herts, AL5 3LN
Tel: 01582 764038
Email: acton_theatreco@yahoo.co.uk
Contact: Susie Scambler, Artistic Director

Action Transport Theatre Company
Whitby Hall, Stanney Lane, Ellesmere Port, South Wirral, CH65 9AE
Tel: 0151 3572120
Contact: Paula Davenport-Ball, General Manager

Arad Goch
Stryd Y Baddon, Aberystwyth, Ceredigion, SY23 2NN
Tel: 01907 617998
Email: jeremy@aradgoch.org
Contact: Jeremy Turner, Artistic Director

ARC Theatre Ensemble
Eastbury Manor House, Eastbury Square, Barking, Essex, IG11 5SN
Tel: 0208 5941095
Email: nita@arcoff.demon.co.uk

Baboro Galway International Children's Festival
Balck Box, Dyke Road, Galway, Ireland
Tel: 353 91 509705
Email: education@gaf.iol.ie

Barking Dog Theatre Company
18 Hayley Bell Gardens, Bishops Stortford, Herts, CM23 3HB
Tel: 01279 465550
Email: pat@barkingdog.co.uk
Contact: Patrick Jacobs, Director

Belgrade Theatre
Head of Young People's Work, Belgrade Square, Coventry, CV1 1GS
Tel: 02476 846721
Contact: Matthew Pegg, Head of Young People's Work

Birmingham Repertory Theatre
Broad Street, Birmingham, B1 2EP
Tel: 0121 2452000
Email: rachel.feneley@birmingham-rep.co.uk
Contact: Rachel Feneley, Head of Education

Booster Cushion Theatre
Building B, 1st Floor, Chocolate Factory, Clarendon Road,
   London N22 6XJ

Bournemouth Theatre in Education
BCCA, 93 Haviland Road, Bournemouth, BH7 6HJ
Tel: 01202 395759
Email: bcca@bournemouth.gov.uk

Bruvvers Theatre Company
Ouseburn Warehouse Workshops, 36 Lime Street, Ouseburn,
   Newcastle-Upon-Tyne, NE1 2PQ
Tel: 0191 2619230
Email: m.mould@can-online.org.uk
Contact: Michael Mould, Director

Chaplins in Education
Head of Production, Units A and B, The Acorn Centre,
   Roebuck Road, Hainault, Essex, IG6 3TU
Tel: 0208 5012121
Contact: Damion Nickerson, Head of Production

Chichester Festival Theatre
Education Director, Oaklands Park, Chichester, W Sussex, PO19 4AP
Tel: 01243 784437
Email: andy.bereton@cft.org.uk
Contact: Andy Bereton

Classworks Theatre
Cambridge Drama Centre, Covent Garden, Cambridge, CB1 2HR
Tel: 01223 461901
Email: info@classworks.org.uk

Cleveland Theatre Company
Arts Centre, Vane Terrace, Darlington, Co Durham, DL3 7AX
Tel: 01325 352004
Email: paul@ctctheatre.org.uk
Contact: Paul Harman, Artistic Director

Cornelius and Jones Productions
49 Carters Close, Sherington, Newport Pagnell,
  Bucks, MK16 9NW
Tel: 01908 612593
Email: admin@corneliusjones.com

Croydon Clocktower
Education Officer, Katherine Street, Croydon, CR9 1ET
Contact: Lisa Mead, Education Officer

Cwmni'r Fran Wen
The Old Primary School, Pentraeth Road, Menai Bridge,
  Anglesey, LL59 5HS
Tel: 01248 715048
Email: cwmnifranwen@aol.com
Contact: Nia Rees Williams, Administrator

Freehand Theatre
1 Reynard Villas, Mayfield Grove, Balidon, Shipley,
  W. Yorshire, BD17 6DY
Tel: 01274 585277
Email: freehandtheatre@pop3.poptel.org.uk
Contact: Lizzie Allen, Co-Director

Futures Theatre Company
St Peter's Centre, Cranfield Road, London SE1 1UF
Tel: 020 8694 0289
Email: futures@ukonline.co.uk
Contact: Caroline Bryant

Gwent Theatre
The Drama Centre, Pen-Y-Pound, Abergavenny,
  Gwent, NP7 5UD
Tel: 01873 853167
Email: gwenttie@aol.com
Contact: Julia Davies, Administrator

Half Moon Young People's Theatre
43 Whitehorse Road, Stepney, London E1 0ND
Tel: 0207 2658138
Email: halfmoon@dircon.co.uk, *website:* www.halfmoon.org.uk
Contact: Chris Elwell, Artistic Director

Hand to Mouth
51 Arnold Road, Southampton, SO17 ITF
Tel: 023 80555392
Email: htmtheatre@btinternet.com,
   website: www.handtomouth.co.uk
Contact: Martin Bridle, Director

Haymarket Theatre Outreach Dept.
Belgrave Gate, Leicester, LE1 3YQ
Tel: 0116 2530021
Email: adel@leicesterhaymarkettheatre.org
Contact: Ellen Bianchini, Education Administrator

Imaginate
5th Floor, 45a George Street, Edinburgh, EH2 2HT
Tel: 0131 2258050
Email: tony@sicf.ednet.co.uk
Contact: Tessa Rennie

Interplay Theatre Company
Armley Ridge Road, Leeds, LS12 3LE
Tel: 0113 2638556
Email: steve@interplaytheatre.org
Contact: Gareth Moss, General Manager

Jack Drum Arts
West New Houses, Baldersdale, Barnard Castle,
   Co Durham, DL12 9UU
Tel: 01833 650623
Email: jill.cole@jackdrum.co.uk
Contact: Jill Cole

Kazzum
BAC, Lavender Hill, Wandsworth, London SW11 5TN
Tel: 0207 2230703
Email: Kazzum@talk 21.com
Contact: Peter Glanville, Artistic Director

Kinetic Theatre
Suite H, Jubilee Centre, Lombard Road, London SW18 3TZ
Tel: 0208 2862613
Email: Sarah@kinetictheatre.co.uk,
   website: www.kinetictheatre.co.uk

Krazy Kat Theatre Company
173 Hartington Road, Brighton, E Sussex, BN2 3PA
Tel: 01723 692552
Email: kkat@demon.co.uk
Contact: Alistair Macmillan, Administrative Director

Lambeth Children's Theatre Company
27 Wigmore Road, London SE24 0AS
Tel: 0207 7335270
Email: lambch@globalnet.co.uk
Contact: Raymond Cook, Director

Lanternfish Theatre Company
16 Claudian Place, St Albans, Herts., AL3 4JE
Tel: 01727 761007
Email: lantern@dircon.co.uk
Contact: Tony Peters

London Bubble
5 Elephant Lane, London SE16 4JD
Tel: 0207 2374434
Email: admin@londonbubble.org.uk

Ludus Dance Agency
Assembly Rooms,, King Street, Lancaster, LA1 1RE
Tel: 01524 847744
Email: ludus@easynet.co.uk, *website:* www.ludus.org
Contact: Gil Graystone, Head of Touring

M6 Theatre Company
Hamer C. P. School, Albert Royds Street, Rochdale,
  Lancs., OL16 2SU
Tel: 01706 355898
Email: info@m6theatre.freeserve.co.uk
Contact: Jane Milne, Administrator

Magic Carpet Theatre
18 Church Street, Sutton-on-Hull, East Riding, HU7 4TS
Tel: 01482 709939
Email: jon@magiccarpettheatre.co.
Contact: Jon Marshall, Director

Man Mela Theatre Company
The Albany, Douglas Way, Deptford, SE8 4AG
Tel: 0208 6920231
Email: man-mela@dircon.co.uk
Contact: Caroline Goffin, Administrator

Mimika Theatre
26 Highbury Terrace, Leeds, W. Yorkshire, LS6 4ET
Tel: 0113 2740053
Email: mimika@btinternet.com
Contact: Jenny Ward, Administrator/Performer

Mirage Children's Theatre Company
Park Walk Primary School, Park Walk, London SW10 0AY
Tel: 0207 3499969
Email: mir-arts@dircon.co.uk
Contact: Frank Brennan, Artistic Director

Oily Cart
Smallwood School Annexe, Smallwood Road, Tooting,
    London SW17 0TW
Tel: 0208 6726329
Email: oilycart@globalnet.co.uk
Contact: Tim Webb, Artistic Director

Old Town Hall Theatre
High Street, Hemel Hempstead, Herts, HP1 3AE
Tel: 01442 228095
Email: paul.russ@dacorum.gov.uk
Contact: Alison Young, General Manager

Oldham MBC Arts and Events
The Museum, Greaves Street, Oldham, Lancashire, OL1 1DN
Tel: 0161 9113097/4076
Email: els.artsandevents@oldham.gov.uk
Contact: Linda Graham, Events Officer

Palace Theatre
Education Department, Clarendon Road, Watford, WD1 1JZ
Tel: 01923 235455
Email: education@watfordtheatre.co.uk
Contact: Hassina Khan, Education Manager

Parasol Theatre
Garden House, 4 Sunnyside, Wimbledon, London SW19 4SL
Tel: 0208 9469478
Contact: Richard Gill, Artistic Director

Piano Music Theatre
160 Victoria Street, London N22 7XQ
Tel: 0208 8886536
Email: baronshouse2000@yahoo.com
Contact: Stephen Baron

Playtime Theatre Company
18 Bennell's Avenue, Whitstable, Kent, CT5 2HP
Tel: 01227 266272
Email: playtime@dircon.co.uk

Polka Theatre for Children
240 The Broadway, Wimbledon, London SW19 1SB
Tel: 0208 5458320
Email: info@polkatheatre.com

Poole Arts Centre
Kingland Road, Poole, Dorset, BH15 1UG
Tel: 01202 665334
Email: helend@pooleartscentre.co.uk
Contact: Helen Donaldson, Programme Manager

Proper Job Theatre Projects
48a Byram Arcade, Westgate, Huddersfield, W. Yorkshire, HD1 1ND
Tel: 01484 514687
Email: mail@properjob.org.uk
Contact: Rhian Jones, Administrator

Quicksilver Theatre
4 Enfield Road, London N1 5AZ
Tel: 0207 2412942
Email: talktous@quicksilvertheatre.org
Contact: Helen Gethin, Admin Director

Red Ladder Theatre Company
3 St Peter's Buildings, York Street, Leeds, W. Yorkshire, LS9 8AJ
Tel: 0113 2455311
Email: wendy@redladder.co.uk
Contact: Wendy Harris, Artistic Director

Replay Productions Ltd
Old Museum Arts Centre, 7 College Square North, Belfast, BT1 6AR
Tel: 02890 322773
Email: replay@dircon.co.uk
Contact: Ali FitzGibbon, Administrator

Ripstop Productions
15 Wildfell Road, London SE6 4HU
Tel: 07041 372177
Email: info@ripstoptheatre.co.uk, *website:* www.ripstoptheatre.co.uk
Contact: Zannie Fraser, Artistic Director

Roundabout Theatre in Education
Nottingham Playhouse, Wellington Circus, Nottingham, NG1 5AF
Tel: 0115 9474361
Email: andrewb@nottinghamplayhouse.co.uk,
    website: www.roundabout.org.uk
Contact: Andrew Breakwell, Director of Roundabout and Education

Royal Lyceum Theatre
Grindlay Street, Edinburgh, EH3 9AX
Tel: 0131 2297404
Email: ssmall@lyceum.org.uk
Contact: Steven Small, Education Development Officer

Shakespeare 4 Kidz
Email: office@shakespeare4kidz.com
Contact: Julian Chenery

Sheffield Theatres TIE
Crucible Theatre, 55 Norfolk Street, Sheffield, S. Yokshire, S1 1DA
Tel: 0114 2495999
Email: sheff-theatres@pop3.poptel.org.uk
Contact: Karen Simpson, Education Director

Sixth Sense
The Burkhardt Hall, Swindon College, Regent Circus,
    Swindon, Wilts, SN1 1PT
Tel: 01793 614864
Email: sstc@dircon.co.uk,
    website: www.sixthsensetheatrecompany.co.uk

Small World Theatre
Fern Villa, Llandygwydd, Cardigan, Ceredigion, SA43 2QX
Tel: 01239 682785
Email: smallworld@enterprise.net
Contact: Ann Shrosbree

Snap People's Theatre Trust
Email: info@snaptheatre.co.uk
Contact: Mike Wood

Spotlites Theatre Company
King's Theatre, 338 High Street, Chatham, Kent, ME4 4NR
Tel: 01634 829468
Email: spotlites@hotmail.com
Contact: Rachel King, Artistic Director

Storybox Theatre
Strawberry Cottages, Priors Court, Meddon Street, Bideford,
North Devon, EX39 2EJ
Tel: 01237 422171
Email: storybox@tantraweb.co.uk
Contact: Tanya Landman, Co-Director

TAG Theatre Company
18 Albion Street, Glasgow, G1 1LH
Tel: 0141 5524949
Email: tag@glasgow.almac.co.uk
Contact: Jon Morgan, General Manager

Take Art!
Unit 10, North Street Workshops, Stoke-sub-Hamdon, Somerset,
TA14 6QR
Tel: 01935 823151
Email: Takeart@dial.pipex.com
Contact: Ralph Lister, Director

Tam Tam Theatre
145 Pepys Road, New Cross, London SE14 5SQ
Tel: 0207 2775874
Email: tamtamtheatre@hotmail.com
Contact: Marleen Vermeulen

The Rose Theatre
Edge Hill Cottage, St Helen's Road, Ormskirk, Lancs, L39 4QP
Email: gibbonsj@edgehill.ac.uk
Contact: June Gibbons

Theatr Iolo
Old School Building, Cefn Road, Mynachdy, Cardiff,
    South Wales, CF14 3HS
Tel: 029 20613782
Email: admin@theatriolo.com, *website:* www.theatriolo.com
Contact: Kevin Lewis, Artistic Director

Theatr Powys
Drama Centre, Tremont Road, Llandrindod Wells, LD1 5EB
Tel: 01579 824444
Email: theatr.powys@powys.gov.uk
Contact: Sophie Anderson, General Manager

Theatre Company Blah Blah Blah!
East Leeds Family Learning Centre, Brooklands View, Seacroft,
    Leeds, W. Yorkshire, LS14 6SA
Tel: 0113 2243171
Email: admin@blahs.co.uk, *website:* www.blahs.co.uk
Contact: Anthony Haddon, Artistic Director

Theate Royal, Bath
Sawcross, Bath, BA1 1ET
Tel: 01225 448815
Email: kate.cross@theatreroyal.org.uk,
    website: www.theatreroyal.org.uk
Contact: Kate Cross, Head of Education

Theatre Royal, Bury St Edmunds
Westgate Street, Bury St Edmunds, Suffolk, IP33 1QR
Tel: 01284 755127
Email: obrienb@theatreroyal.org
Contact: Bridget O'Brien, Education Officer

Theatre Venture
Stratford Circus, Theatre Square, Stratford, London E15 1BX
Tel: 0208 519 6678
Email: info@theatre-venture.org, *website:* www.theatre-venture.org
Contact: Ben Ayrton, Artistic Director

Theatre-Rites
23 Windsor Road, London N7 6JG
Tel: 0207 6860771
Email: info@theatre-rites.demon.co.uk
Contact: Penny Bernand, Artistic Director

Tiebreak Theatre Company
Heartsease High School, Marryat Road, Norwich, NR7 9DF
Tel: 01603 435209
Email: info@tiebreak-theatre.com,
    website: www.tiebreak-theatre.com

Travelling Light Theatre Company
13 West Street, Old Market, Bristol, BS2 0DF
Tel: 0117 3773166
Email: info@travlight.co.uk, *website:* www.travlight.co.uk
Contact: Jude Merrill, Artistic Producer

Unicorn Theatre for Children
St Mark's Studios, Chillingworth Road, London N7 8QJ
Tel: 0207 7000702
Email: admin@unicorntheatre.com
Contact: Tony Graham, Artistic Director

Walk the Plank
The Wheelhouse, 72 Broad Street, Salford, M6 5BZ
Tel: 0161 7368964
Email: info@walktheplank.co.uk
Contact: Liz Pugh, Producer

Warwick Arts Centre
University of Warwick, Coventry, CV4 7AL
Tel: 024 76524252
Email: b.c.bishop@warwick.ac.uk
Contact: Brian Bishop, Education Liaison Officer

West Yorkshire Playhouse
Playhouse Square, Quarry Hill, Leeds, LS2 7UP
Tel: 0113 2442141
Email: gailm@wyp.org.uk
Contact: Gail McIntyre, Director, Schools Company